Murano ★8

Torcello 25★

D0356584

19 Santa Maria dei Miracoli

21 Santi Giovanni e Paolo

Santa Maria Formosa 17

23 Scuola di San Giorgio degli Schiavoni

1 Basilica di San Marco

16 San Zaccaria

11 Campanile

10 Palazzo Ducale

San Zaccaria (Piazza San Marco)

San Marco (MVE)

Arsenale

14 San Giorgio Maggiore

San Giorgio

J   K   L

Fodor's
25BEST
Venice

by Tim Jepson

Fodor's Travel Publications
New York • Toronto • London • Sydney • Auckland
www.fodors.com

Contents

KEY TO SYMBOLS

- ✚ Map reference to the accompanying fold-out map
- ✉ Address
- ☎ Telephone number
- 🕓 Opening/closing times
- 🍽 Restaurant or café
- 🚉 Nearest rail station
- 🚌 Nearest bus route
- ⛴ Nearest riverboat or ferry stop

ENTERTAINMENT 130

Whether you're after a cultural fix or just want a place to relax with a drink after a hard day's sightseeing, we've made the best choices for you.

EAT 140

Uncover great dining experiences, from a quick bite at lunch to top-notch evening meals.

SLEEP 152

We've brought together the best hotels in the city, whatever budget you're on.

NEED TO KNOW 160

The practical information you need to make your trip run smoothly.

PULL-OUT MAP

The pull-out map accompanying this book is a comprehensive street plan of the city. We've given grid references within the book for each sight and listing.

🚹 Facilities for visitors with disabilities

🅱 Tourist information

🅱 Other practical information

▷ Further information

🔖 Admission charges: Expensive (over €8), Moderate (€5–€8) and Inexpensive (under €5)

Introducing Venice

Venice has been seducing visitors for centuries, its impossible watery setting and fairy-tale appearance casting a spell whose potency remains undiminished by floods, mass tourism and the many other travails of the modern world.

The city sits at the heart of a lagoon, its many islands, alleys and canals divided into six districts, or *sestieri*, three to the west of the Canal Grande (San Polo, Dorsoduro and Santa Croce) and three to the east (San Marco, Castello and Cannaregio). Each has its own unmissable sights and each has a maze of timeless alleys and streets—a delight to wander for their own sake.

This labyrinth may look intimidating, but the city is easier to navigate than it looks: Distances are short, a few key streets wend through the maze, and the Rialto, Venice's old commercial heart, and the Piazza San Marco, its most famous square, provide central points of reference. On your first morning, though, resist the temptation to dash for the major sights. Start instead with a cappuccino in a sleepy square, or something where the crowds don't turn you away from the city at the first acquaintance.

Then you can move to the bigger draws and finally grapple with what to see among Venice's plethora of wonderful churches, palaces and museums. Don't forget the cafés, walks, tiny shops and essential boat trips along the Canal Grande or perhaps out to the islands of the lagoon.

However, in seeing the sights, don't fall into the trap of believing Venice is a sort of medieval theme park, a dead city sustained for the benefit of visitors. The population may be falling, but this is an enduring place; a city where people live and work, raise their families and have the same hopes and worries as people everywhere else. Where they differ is in living their everyday lives surrounded by the glories of one of the world's most beautiful cities. The pride they feel in this manifests itself in very diverse ways, but it's indubitably this pride that will preserve the city and its treasures for generations to come.

FACTS AND FIGURES

- It is estimated that there are 3,000 alleys in Venice. Laid end to end they would stretch for 192km (120 miles)
- Venice has around 400 bridges
- The city has some 450 souvenir shops
- Fifty per cent of the city's workforce is involved in tourism
- In 1946 the population of central Venice was 110,000; today, it's below 60,000

SPECIAL TICKETS

The Museum Pass (€18) gives entry to all civic museums including the Palazzo Ducale. The Musei di Piazza San Marco ticket (April–1 Nov €13; 2 Nov–Mar €12) gives entry to all museums on Piazza San Marco and one other civic museum (restrictions in winter). A ticket for the Chorus Group of 16 artistically important churches is €10, or €3 for a single church.

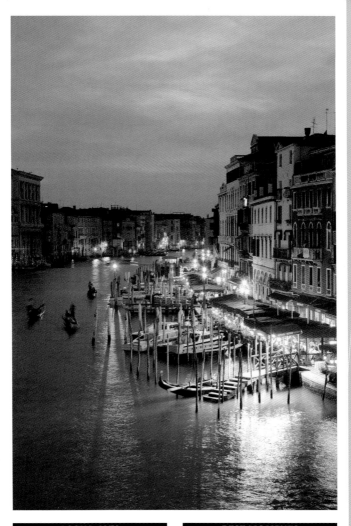

ACQUA ALTA

Visit Venice between November and April and you run the risk of encountering *acqua alta* or 'high water', when winter weather, winds and high tides combine to submerge large areas. Raised wooden walkways, *passarelle*, are laid out on key routes to help people get around, and packing some waterproof footwear is a good idea.

BEST MOMENTS

These are often away from the main sights. So take a boat along the Canal Grande just for the ride, or see the Rialto markets at the crack of dawn before the crowds arrive. Little beats an aerial view, preferably from the top of San Giorgio Maggiore, and no city offers more to those who wander at random. A trip to the islands off-season can be magical.

Focus On a Thousand Years of Tourism

An incredible 17 million tourists now visit Venice every year. That's a lot of people, but Venice has always attracted myriad visitors, who've been staring open-mouthed at her watery beauties for well over 1,000 years.

The First Visitors

Early visitors were traders, attracted to this mercantile city, standing at the western end of the Silk Road and at the crossroads of East and West. Venice was renowned as the place to source the ultimate in luxury goods, and merchants came from all over Europe with shopping lists from the wealthy of the time. They fulfilled their orders and carried home stories of this incredible city.

By the 12th century, foreigners, often en route to the East, were coming to Venice for the express purpose of visiting the city. They were welcomed with open arms, the pragmatic and business-like Venetians viewing them as merely another commodity, not to be traded, but certainly to be housed, fed and watered at considerable profit—an activity that's pursued to this day.

Europe's Party Capital

By the 18th century Venice was known as Europe's party capital par excellence. Those 18th-century equivalents of gap-year students, the Grand Tourists, flocked to the city, sending their parents reports of churches visited and art admired, while in reality throwing themselves into the hedonistic charms of a carnival season that literally stretched for more than six months of the year. Everyone was masked, no one recognizable, anything permissible.

The prostitutes were the most renowned in Europe, publishing their own guidebook to the city's brothels and flaunting their charms in a daily gondola parade down the Rio della Sensa. They were less open about the

Clockwise from top: A costumed couple walk near Piazza San Marco During Carnavale; boats taking part in the Regata Storica on the Canal Grande in

incidence of syphilis in Venice; it's estimated that by the 18th century around 20 per cent of the population, including the tourists, suffered from the disease.

The 19th Century

Things calmed down considerably in the 19th century; in 1797 the Republic fell and Venice became a provincial backwater. Tourists were obsessed with the romantic, and the decaying beauty of Venice was nothing if not romantic. English poets Byron, Robert Browning, Percy Bysshe Shelley and the American writer Henry James all spent time here, and art critic and author John Ruskin wrote evocatively about the city, creating an image of Venice as the ultimate romantic destination.

Tourism Today

Today things have moved on again and the tourist profile has changed out of all recognition. Some 80 per cent of visitors are day trippers, pouring in across the causeway and, increasingly, from the super-size cruise ships that include Venice on their itineraries. Their Venetian experience may be short and their numbers huge, but the council is doing its best to ensure modern visitors leave with unforgettable and positive memories.

The key lies in balancing the numbers; the steady flow of tourists means that the visitor numbers can be spread out over the year so the city isn't so overwhelmed. The Venice Connected initiative is a financial inducement to persuade visitors to come during the winter months, when prices are lower and crowds smaller. It's important, too, that tourists know that the mooring and parking fees paid by tour operators go to help preserve this marvellous city, while every euro spent on eating and shopping contributes to keeping the city functioning as something more than a living museum.

September; a detail of the Gothic tracery on the facade of Ca' d'Oro; the striking Basilica di San Marco; Riva degli Schiavoni gondola pier; Piazza San Marco at night

Top Tips For...

These great suggestions will help you tailor your ideal visit to Venice, no matter how you choose to spend your time.

...Fabulous Views
Take the elevator to the top of the **Campanile** (▷ 34–35) for spectacular, far-reaching views over the rooftops.
The bell tower of **San Giorgio Maggiore** (▷ 40–41) offers sweeping vistas across the entire city.
Climb the tower of the cathedral on **Torcello** (▷ 62–63) for a sweeping panorama of the Venetian lagoon.

...Burning the Midnight Oil
Have a drink in one of the cafés and bars on **Campo Santa Margherita** (▷ 67).
Find a fusty old *enoteca* (wine bar) such as **Do Mori** (▷ 136).
Venice has few late-opening nightspots—**Vino Vino** (▷ 139) and **Paradiso Perduto** (▷ 137) are two of the best.

...The Lap of Luxury
Splash out on one of Venice's new-wave designer hotels – **Ca' Maria Adele** (▷ 157) typifies this fabulous self-indulgence.
Enjoy an expensive coffee or, better, an aperitif or late drink in **Caffè Florian** (▷ 147), a Venetian institution.
Go to a celebrity bar. It's crowded and a bit touristy, but **Harry's Bar** (▷ 148) still serves a fine cocktail.

...A Breath of Fresh Air
The tiny **Giardini ex Reali** (▷ 68) offers a little green space close to San Marco.
Visit **Torcello** (▷ 62–63) for some bracing sea air.
Verdant **Sant'Erasmo** (▷ 76), Venice's vegetable garden, offers great opportunities for fresh air and country walking.

Clockwise from top: A view down onto Piazza San Marco from the Campanile; Canal Grande seen from the Ponte dell'Accademia; inside a shop selling

...Keeping the Children Happy

Take them on plenty of boat rides, especially down the Canal Grande (▷ 18–19).
Buy them a mask from **Mondo Novo** (▷ 127) or ice cream from **Nico** (▷ 149) or **GROM** (▷ 148).
Visit one of Murano's glass factories to see glassblowers in action (▷ 28–29).

...Saving for a Rainy Day

Buy the **Chorus Pass** (€10) for reduced admission to some of Venice's finest churches (▷ panel, 4).
For the price of a boat ticket you can travel the length of the **Canal Grande**, surely the world's finest journey by public transportation (▷ 18–19, 166–167).
Just €0.60 on a *traghetto* (▷ 167) across the Canal Grande buys you a ride on a gondola.

...Specialty Shopping

Many of Venice's high-fashion and other designer stores cluster in and around Calle Larga XXII Marzio. Check out **Prada** (▷ 129), one of the biggest and most popular names in Italian fashion.
For superb food shopping nothing beats the **Rialto markets** (▷ 39, 128) and the delicatessens in the surrounding streets such as Ruga Vecchia di San Giovanni.
Small, specialist stores line the **Mercerie** (▷ 69) and other streets between St. Mark's and the Rialto Bridge. Marbled paper, glass and local foods are popular choices.

...An Evening on the Town

Take in an opera or concert at **La Fenice** (▷ 75, 138), Venice's opera house.
Contact the tourist office (▷ 167) to find **a concert** in one of Venice's churches or palaces.
Dress up for an evening's lighthearted gambling in Venice's **casino** (▷ 135).

handmade paper; a fruit stall at the Rialto market;
Teatro La Fenice; the sumptuous surroundings of
Caffè Florian; the green fields on Torcello island

Timeline

800BC Sporadic settlement of the lagoon by the Venetii and Euganei tribes.

250BC Rome conquers Venetia and founds important colonies at Padua, Verona, Altinium and Aquileia.

MARCO POLO

Born in Venice in 1254, Marco Polo left with his father in 1269 on a journey that would last two decades. In 1275 he arrived at the court of Kublai Khan, where he served the Mongol emperor until 1295. In 1298 he was captured by the Genoese and it was from prison that he dictated his *Description of the World*.

ANTONIO VIVALDI

Vivaldi was born in Venice in 1678. Although ordained as a priest, he devoted his life to music, teaching violin at La Pietà orphanage, whose girls received music training as part of their state-funded education. La Pietà's orchestra enabled Vivaldi to create a wealth of musical compositions, including his most famous work *The Four Seasons*.

AD402 Alaric the Goth sacks Altinium and other northeastern colonies. A vision of the Virgin guides refugees to an island in the lagoon.

421 According to legend Venice is founded on 25 March, the Feast Day of the Virgin Mary.

453 Aquileia is sacked by Attila the Hun, prompting another exodus of refugees to the lagoon.

697 The first Doge (leader) of Venice, Paoluccio Anafesto, is elected.

810 Lagoon dwellers gather on the more easily defended islands of the Rialto.

828 Venetian merchants steal the relics of St. Mark from Alexandria.

1171 Venice's six districts are founded.

1204 Venice sacks Constantinople and acquires much of the former Byzantine Empire.

The Doge sets out in the Bucentaur for the ceremony of Marriage to the Sea (▷ 162)

Piazza San Marco after flooding

1380 Victory over the Genoese at the Battle of Chioggia. Venice wins naval supremacy in the Adriatic and Mediterranean.

1406 Venice defeats Padua and Verona to lay the foundations of a mainland empire.

1453 Venice's power is at its height but the Turks take Constantinople. Over the next 200 years they take Cyprus and Crete.

1498 The discovery of the Cape route to the East weakens Venice's trading monopolies.

1718 Loss of Morea marks the end of Venice's maritime empire.

1797 Napolean invades Italy: the last doge abdicates and the Venetian Republic comes to an end.

1814 After Napolean's defeat, the Congress of Vienna cedes Venice and the Veneto to Austria.

1866 Venice joins a united Italy.

1966 Devastating floods draw international attention to the decay of Venice's buildings and artistic treasures; start of major fund-raising for restoration.

2003 Work on MOSE flood barrier at lagoon entrances goes ahead.

2007 Ponte della Costituzione, bridge over Canal Grande, opens.

2011 Annual tourist numbers top 17 million; city population falls below 60,000.

COURTESANS AND VENETIAN GREED

At the end of the 16th century, the city contained 11,654 women of the night. This compared with 2,889 patrician women; 1,936 burghers; and 2,508 nuns. Taxes from prostitution funded an estimated 12 galleys (ships). In the 18th century, according to one contemporary report, 'Venetians did not taste their pleasures, but swallowed them whole'. Another observer wrote that 'the men are women, the women are men, and all are monkeys'.

Marco Polo, the great Venetian-born traveller

Crossing Ponte della Costituzione

Top 25

This section contains the must-see Top 25 sights and experiences in Venice. They are listed alphabetically, and numbered so you can locate them on the inside front cover map.

1 Basilica di San Marco

- Central door
- Facade mosaics
- Bronze horses
- Rood screen
- Mosaic pavement
- Pala d'Oro
- Interior mosaics

TIPS

- Dress code: no shorts; women must cover shoulders and upper arms.
- To avoid long lines go in early or late afternoon.

Don't allow yourself to be discouraged by the teeming crowds that engulf the Basilica di San Marco, as ultimately no one can remain unimpressed by what is surely one of the world's greatest medieval buildings.

St. Mark's resting place The basilica was begun in 832 to house the body of St. Mark, stolen from Alexandria by Venetian merchants four years earlier. For almost 1,000 years it served as the doge's private 'chapel' and the city's spiritual heart, accumulating the decorative fruits of a millennium to emerge as the most exotic hybrid of Western and Byzantine architecture in Europe. The original building (destroyed by rioting) was replaced in 978 and again in 1094, the church from the latter date making up most of the one you see today.

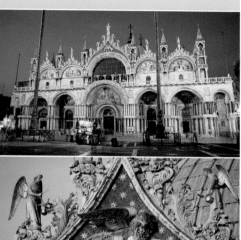

Clockwise from far left: The decorated facade above the main door of the basilica; the interior is decorated with mosaics depicting the basilica itself; the basilica lit up at night-time; a rooftop detail of the Winged Lion, a symbol of St. Mark

Time to explore Admiring the basilica's treasures is exhausting because there are so many, and because the almost constant crowds make exploring a dispiriting business. The building remains overwhelmingly striking; spend a few minutes taking in some of the exterior details before plunging inside. These include the *Translation of the Body of St. Mark to the Basilica* (1260–70) above the leftmost door, the west facade's only original mosaic (the rest are later copies) and the superb Romanesque carvings (1240–65) above the central door. Inside, see the famous bronze horses (probably third century AD) in the upper gallery, the view from the Loggia dei Cavalli, the treasury (full of antique silverware), and the Pala d'Oro, an altar screen encrusted with more than 2,600 pearls, rubies, emeralds and other precious stones.

THE BASICS

www.basilicasanmarco.it

➕ J6

✉ Piazza San Marco 1, San Marco 30124

☎ 041 522 5205, 041 522 5697, 041 270 8311

🕐 Apr–Oct Mon–Sat 9.45–5.30, Sun 2–4; Nov–Mar 9.45–4.30, Sun 2–4

🍴 Piazza San Marco

�C All services to San Marco Vallaresso, San Marco Giardinetti or San Zaccaria

♿ Some steps; uneven floors

💶 Basilica free. Treasury and Pala d'Oro expensive

HIGHLIGHTS

- Canal Grande facade
- *Massacre of the Innocents*, artist unknown
- *Crucifixion*, Antonio Vivarini
- *St. Sebastian*, Andrea Mantegna
- *Man and Woman*, busts by Tullio Lombardo
- *The Story of the True Cross*, bronze reliefs by Andrea Briscio
- *Madonna*, Giovanni Bellini
- *Flagellation*, Luca Signorelli

The smaller and less famous galleries of a city are often the most rewarding. The Ca' d'Oro's collection of paintings, sculptures and objets d'art is one of the most absorbing in Venice.

Palace The Ca' d'Oro, or 'House of Gold', takes its name from the gilding that once covered its facade, a decorative veneer now worn away by wind and rain. However, the facade remains one of the most accomplished pieces of Venetian-Byzantine architecture in the city. The same, sadly, cannot be said of the interior, which has been ravaged by hapless owners.

Exhibits Galleria Franchetti, named for the owner who gave his home and collection to the state in 1916, divides into two floors, each arranged around a central *portego*. On the lower floor a captivating polyptych of the *Crucifixion* by Antonio Vivarini greets you, along with sculptural fragments belonging to the *Massacre of the Innocents* (14th century). Moving right you come to the gallery's pictorial masterpiece, Mantegna's sombre *St. Sebastian* (1506). To its left, in the *portego*, is a pair of busts by Tullio Lombardo (15th century), followed by six bronze reliefs, *The Story of the True Cross*, by Andrea Briscio (1470–1532). The rooms off the *portego* contain medallions, a Madonna by Giovanni Bellini and a range of Florentine and Sienese paintings.

More art Upstairs there are tapestries, paintings by Titian, Van Dyck and Tintoretto, and damaged frescoes by Pordenone, Titian and Giorgione.

THE BASICS

www.polomuseale.venezia.beniculturali.it

🔡 G4

✉ Calle di Ca' d'Oro, Cannaregio 3932, off Strada Nova

☎ 041 520 0345

🕓 Mon 8.15–2, Tue–Sun 8.15–7.15

🚢 Ca' d'Oro N, 1

♿ Poor: stairs

💶 Moderate

HIGHLIGHTS

● Ballroom
● G. B. Tiepolo ceiling frescoes
● Carriera portraits
● Lacquerwork
● Gondola cabin, or *felze*
● Canaletto paintings
● Francesco Guardi paintings
● Pietro Longhi paintings
● G. D. Tiepolo satirical frescoes

Gazing at the Canal Grande's palaces from a boat you can't help but wish to see inside some of them, which is the attraction of Ca' Rezzonico, a museum that recreates a Venetian palace as it might have been in the 18th century.

How it began The Ca' Rezzonico was begun in 1667 by Baldassare Longhena, a leading architect of his day, but remained half-finished. In 1751 the shell was bought by the Rezzonico family and passed through several hands before opening as a museum in 1936. It begins in fine style in the sumptuous ball-room with *trompe-l'œil* and huge chandeliers. Highlights of rooms include ceiling frescoes by G. B. Tiepolo, fine lacquerwork, Flemish tapestries and pastel portraits by Rosalba Carrera.

Left: Detail of The Banquet at Casa Nani, Given in Honour of their Guest, Clemente Augusto, Elector Archbishop of Cologne, on 9th September 1755 *by Pietro Longhi in the gallery's collection; below: The exterior of the building seen from the Canal Grande*

The collection Much of the palace is devoted to a picture gallery, whose highlight is some paintings by Canaletto, three of only a handful that remain on public display in Venice. Also of interest are Francesco Guardi's views of the city's convents and gambling rooms, together with 39 amateurish but fascinating portraits of Venetian life by Pietro Longhi. Among them his well-known *Rhinoceros*, painted during the animal's stay in Venice in 1779. Rooms off to the right include a splendid bed-chamber, complete with 18th-century closet and sponge-bag. Of special note are a series of satirical frescoes (1793–97) by G. D. Tiepolo, a collection of traditional puppets, three rooms from an old pharmacy, fine clothing enhanced with lace and the excellent views from the palace's upper floors.

THE BASICS

www.museiciviciveneziani.it
✚ E6
✉ Fondamenta Rezzonico, Dorsoduro 3136
☎ 041 241 0100
🕓 Apr–Oct Wed–Mon 10–6; Nov–Mar 10–5. Ticket office closes 1 hour earlier
🍴 Campo San Barnaba
🚤 Ca' Rezzonico 1
♿ Good
💰 Expensive
❓ Museum Pass (▷ 4)

4 Canal Grande

HIGHLIGHTS

- Palazzo Vendramin-Calergi
- San Stae
- Ca' Pesaro (▷ 66–67)
- Ca' d'Oro (▷ 16–17)
- Ponte di Rialto
- Ca' Rezzonico (▷ 18–19)
- Santa Maria della Salute (▷ 52–53)

TIPS

- The *vaporetto* is probably the best way of seeing the canal; gondolas and taxis are far more expensive.
- If time is short take the No. 2, which has fewer stops than the No. 1.

The world's most beautiful 'street' offers an endlessly unfolding pageant with superb views of the city's finest palaces and a fascinating insight into Venetian life.

A riot of life and noise Snaking 4km (2.5 miles) through the heart of Venice, it divides the city: Three of the city's six districts, or *sestieri*, lie to one side and three to the other. At most hours of the day and night it is alive with boats and bustle, providing an almost hypnotic spectacle when admired from one of its three bridges (the Scalzi, Rialto and Accademia) or from the heavily laden *vaporetti* that ply up and down its length. In addition to the life of the canal is the attraction of the palaces that line its banks, an historical digest of the city's most appealing architecture dating

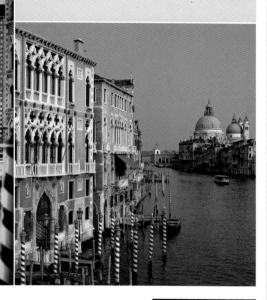

Far left: A busy stretch along the Canal Grande; middle: Lights sparkle on the waters on the canal; below: Looking along the canal past striped gondola poles towards Santa Maria della Salute

back over 500 years. From the Ponte di Rialto, Venice's most famous bridge, you get a view of the canal at its most frantically busy.

Jump on board A trip along this intriguing canal is a pleasure in itself. Board *vaporetto* No. 1 or No. 2 at Piazzale Roma or the Ferrovia (rail station), making sure the boat is heading in the right direction. For the best views, try to secure one of the few outside seats at the front or rear of the boat: Venetians prefer to stand in the middle. The Rialto and Accademia bridges make convenient breaks in the ride, but for your first trip go all the way to San Marco (and then do the return trip to take in the glory of the palaces on the opposite bank). It is also well worth making the trip at night, when the experience, if anything, is even more magical.

THE BASICS

+ D4–G7
🚂 1, 2 (year-round)
♿ Good
🖐 Moderate
❓ *Vaporetto* 1 halts at every stop; 2 stops at Piazzale Roma, Ferrovia, San Marcuola, Rialto, Sant'Angelo, San Tomà, San Samuele, Accademia, San Marco Vallaresso and San Marco Giardinetti

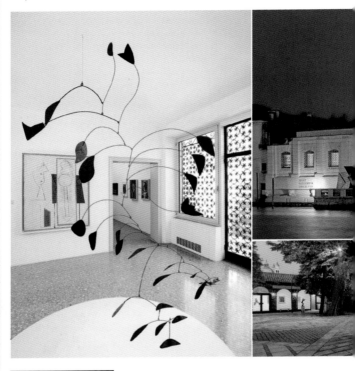

HIGHLIGHTS

- The New Wing
- Henry Moore sculptures
- *Bird in Space*, Constantin Brancusi
- *Red Tower*, De Chirico
- *Robing of the Bride*, Max Ernst
- Silver bedhead, Alexander Calder
- Jackson Pollock paintings
- *The Poet*, Pablo Picasso
- *Angel of the Citadel*, Marino Marini

It is apt that the Accademia and Guggenheim, Venice's two most visited galleries, are close together, juxtaposing two matchless collections—one traditional and one modern.

Perfect setting The Guggenheim's small but polished collection was accumulated by Peggy Guggenheim (1898–1979), daughter of an American copper magnate, and installed by her in the 18th-century Palazzo Venier dei Leoni. The collection's appeal owes much to its immaculate presentation as well as to the beauty of its setting, many of the sculptures being arranged in a lovely garden. This has works by Henry Moore, Paolozzi, Giacometti and others, and houses the New Wing and appealing 'Museum Store'.

Clockwise from far left: Mobile (Arc of Petals) 1941 *by Alexander Calder; the gallery is housed in Palazzo Venier dei Leoni; the Gianno Mattoli Collection; the Nasher Sculpture Garden*

Modern art Guggenheim's taste and money allowed her to select high-quality works from virtually every modern-art movement of the 20th century. At the same time she had a penchant for the surreal and avant-garde, having enjoyed a brief relationship with the German Surrealist painter Max Ernst. The collection features Cubist works by Picasso and Braque, and the Surrealism of Dalí, Magritte and Mirò. American modernists include Jackson Pollock and Mark Rothko, while the English are represented by Francis Bacon. There are sculptures by Calder and Brancusi, as well as works by Italian Futurists Balla and Boccioni from the Gianni Mattioli Collection. The most memorable work is Marino Marini's provocative *Angel of the Citadel*, on the terrace overlooking the Canal Grande.

THE BASICS

www.guggenheim-venice.it

➕ G7

✉ Palazzo Venier dei Leoni, Calle San Cristoforo, Dorsoduro 704

☎ 041 240 5411

🕐 Wed–Mon 10–6

🚤 Salute 1

♿ Good

💶 Expensive

HIGHLIGHTS

● *Madonna and Saints*, Giovanni Bellini
● *Tempest*, Giorgione
● *Supper in the House of Levi*, Veronese
● *The Translation of the Body of St. Mark*, Tintoretto
● *Pietà*, Titian
● Pietro Longhi paintings
● 'The Miracles of the True Cross'
● 'Life of St. Ursula', Carpaccio

TIPS

● Try to avoid Sunday and arrive early if you can.
● English-language tours are available.

Art awaits you at every turn in this city, but you would miss a key experience without a visit to the Accademia, home to the world's greatest collection of Venetian paintings.

Masterpieces The Accademia began life as Venice's art school in 1750, moving to its present site in 1807 when it garnered much of its permanent collection from churches and religious houses suppressed by Napoleonic decree. The building has undergone a lengthy and comprehensive restoration and extension. Some of the gallery's best-known paintings are its Byzantine works, a style that influenced the city's earliest painters. Canvases by Carpaccio, Mantegna, Bellini and others reflect Venice's Renaissance heyday, alongside the Accademia's most famous painting, Giorgione's mysterious

Clockwise from far left: Madonna and Child with Saints Francis, John the Baptist, Job, Dominic, Sebastian and Louis *by Giovanni Bellini; a detail of* Maddona and Child *by Antonio Vivarini; people waiting to enter the gallery; works by Tintoretto and Veronese in one of the rooms*

Tempest (c.1500). High Renaissance masterpieces include Veronese's *Supper in the House of Levi* (1573) and Tintoretto's iconoclastic *Miracle of the Slave* and *The Translation of the Body of St. Mark* (c.1560).

Cycles Leave plenty of time for the Accademia's highlights, two *storie*, or fresco cycles. The first, 'The Miracles of the True Cross' (1494–1510), was painted by a variety of artists for the Scuola di San Giovanni Evangelista. Each describes a miracle worked by a relic of the 'True Cross' owned by the *scuola*, though often the miracle itself takes second place to the fascinating anecdotal detail. The same is true for the second cycle, painted by Carpaccio for the Scuola di Sant' Orsola, with episodes from the 'Life of St. Ursula'.

THE BASICS

www.gallerieaccademia.org
F7
Campo della Carità, Dorsoduro 1050
041 522 2247; reservations 041 250 0345
Tue–Sun 8.15–7.15, Mon 8.15–2
Campo Santo Stefano
Accademia N, 1, 2, 3, 4
Poor: some steps
Expensive

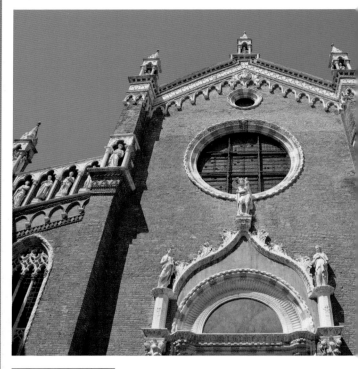

HIGHLIGHTS

- Facade
- Doorway
- *St. Christopher*, Nicolò di Giovanni
- Campanile
- *St. John the Baptist*, Cima da Conegliano
- *Presentation of the Virgin*, Tintoretto
- *The Making of the Golden Calf*, Tintoretto
- *Last Judgement*, Tintoretto
- *St. Agnes Raising Licinius*, Tintoretto (Cappella Contarini)

Madonna dell'Orto ranks high among the many superb Venetian churches; its lovely setting off the tourist trail and graceful red-brick facade are complemented by an airy interior filled with appealing works of art.

Exterior The first church on the present site was founded in 1350 and dedicated to St. Christopher, a statue of whom still dominates the lovely brick and marble facade. The building was rededicated to the Virgin in 1377, an act that was inspired by a miracle-working statue of the Madonna found in a nearby vegetable garden *(orto)*. The elegant doorway, by Bartolomeo Bon, is a Renaissance-tinged work. Note the onion dome of the campanile, clear witness to the Byzantine influence on Venetian architecture.

Left: The brick and marble facade of the Madonna dell'Orto; below: Many of the paintings inside are by Tintoretto who, along with his children, is buried in the church

Interior grandeur Inside, the two aisles contain notable works. The artistic highlights begin in the Contarini Chapel above the first altar on the right, which has Cima da Conegliano's *St. John the Baptist* (1493). At the end of the right nave, above the door, stands Tintoretto's dramatic *Presentation of the Virgin* (1551). In the chapel to the right of the choir lies Tintoretto's tomb (he lived near the church), together with those of his children, Domenico and Marietta. A wall separates the artist from two of his finest paintings, the choir's grand *Last Judgment* and *The Making of the Golden Calf*. Of the three paintings in the apse to the rear, those on the right and left—the *Beheading of St. Paul* and *St. Peter's Vision of the Cross*—are by Tintoretto; the central *Annunciation* is by Palma il Giovane.

THE BASICS

www.chorusvenezia.org

✚ G2

✉ Campo Madonna dell'Orto, Cannaregio 3520

☎ 041 275 0494 or 041 275 0462

🕐 Mon–Sat 10–5, Sun 1–5

🚤 Orto 41, 42, 51, 52

♿ Good

🎟 Inexpensive

❓ Chorus Pass (▷ 4)

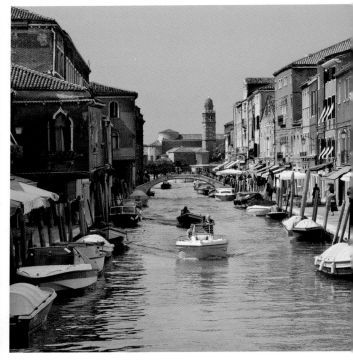

HIGHLIGHTS

- Glass factories
- Museo del Vetro
- Santa Maria e Donato

The lagoon island of Murano is a miniature Venice, and has been the heart of Venetian glass production for over 800 years, at its peak between the 15th and 16th centuries.

Seeing Murano It's a 10-minute trip across the lagoon to Murano, a self-contained community with its own Canal Grande, fine churches, *palazzi* and glass-blowing industry. There are numerous privately run excursions from the city, but for good value and flexibility make the trip independently via the *vaporetti*. Allow two to three hours for a thorough visit. It's quite feasible, given an early start, to combine a visit to Murano with a trip to the northern islands of Burano and Torcello; study the *vaporetto* timetable with care as onward connections run half-hourly only.

Clockwise from left: A canal on the island of Murano; the colonnaded facade of the Basilica dei Santi Maria e Donato; a glass-making factory

Highlights The glass factories are well worth a visit but bear in mind the majority are closed on Saturday and Sunday. A glass-making hub since 1291, Murano has three major sights over and above its ubiquitous glass workshops and showrooms. The first is the church of San Pietro Martire noted for Giovanni Bellini's altarpiece. Also well worth seeing is the Museo del Vetro, Italy's only glass museum, with displays of objects dating from Roman times. Just beyond lies the church of Santa Maria e Donato, distinguished by a striking arched and colonnaded apse. Inside, the 12th-century apse mosaic of the Madonna is outstanding, as are the swirling tinted patterns of the lovely mosaic floor (1141). Don't miss the opportunity to visit a glass workshop or showroom, although you might be tempted by items on sale.

THE BASICS

✚ b2
✉ Isola di Murano
🚢 13, 41, 42, DM, LN from Piazzale Roma, Ferrovia and Fondamenta Nove

Museo del Vetro

✚ b2
✉ Fondamenta Giustinian 8
☎ 041 739 586
🕐 Apr–Oct daily 10–6; Nov–Mar 10–5. Ticket office closes 30 min earlier
🖐 Moderate
🚢 Museo

Santa Maria e Donato

✚ c2
✉ Campo San Donato
🕐 Mon–Sat 9–12, 3.30–7, Sun 3.30–7
🖐 Free
🚢 Museo

HIGHLIGHTS

- Aerial view of Venice (1500), Jacopo de' Barbari
- *Daedalus and Icarus*, Canova
- *Two Women*, Carpaccio
- *The Man in the Red Hat*, Lorenzo Lotto (attributed)
- *Pietà*, Antonello da Messina
- *Madonna and Child*, Giovanni Bellini

Probably only a fraction of the visitors thronging Piazza San Marco venture into the Museo Civico Correr. Those who do not are missing one of Venice's finest museums and picture gallery collections.

Fascinating overview Much of the collection here was accumulated by Abbot Teodoro Correr, a Venetian worthy, and bequeathed to the city in 1830. Today, it spreads over three floors, devoted respectively to historical displays, an art gallery and the small Museo del Risorgimento (covering the 19th-century unification of Italy). The key rooms have lovely old prints and paintings of the city, followed by salons devoted to episodes of Venetian history. Particularly outstanding are the rooms of costumes and hats, standards, armour, globes,

Far left: A fresco of three dancing girls decorates the interior; middle: An impressive gallery; below: Doge Giovanni Mocenigo by Gentile Bellini (c. 1478)

old weapons and ships' instruments. Perhaps the most memorable section, however, is the footwear display showing the famous 'platform' shoes once worn by Venetian ladies of rank.

More art One of the main sections of the museum consists of a large hall devoted to several fine sculptures by Antonio Canova. Occupying the top floor is the city's second-finest art gallery after the Accademia. Its most popular picture is Carpaccio's *Two Women* (1507), a masterful study of ennui once known as *The Courtesans* for the plunging necklines. Other well-known paintings include *The Man in the Red Hat* (by either Carpaccio or Lorenzo Lotto) and a *Pietà* by Antonello da Messina, and works by Cosmè Tura, Alvise Vivarini, and Jacopo, Giovanni and Gentile Bellini.

THE BASICS

www.museicivicivenezani.it

⊞ H6

⊠ Procuratie Nuove, Ala Napoleonica, Piazza San Marco 52, San Marco 30124

☎ 041 240 5211

⏰ Apr–Oct daily 10–7; Nov–Mar 10–5. Ticket office closes 1 hour earlier

🍽 Piazza San Marco

🚢 San Marco Vallaresso, San Marco Giardinetti N, 1, 2

♿ Poor

🎫 Expensive (joint Piazza San Marco ticket)

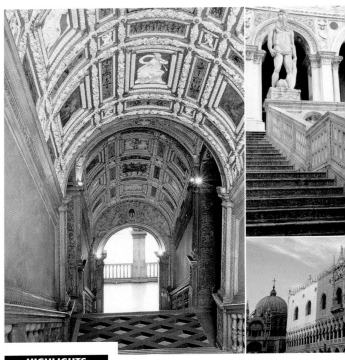

HIGHLIGHTS

- Bridge of Sighs
- Tetrarchs
- Porta della Carta
- Scala dei Giganti
- Arco Foscari
- Sala dell'Anticollegio
- Sala del Collegio
- Sala del Maggior Consiglio
- Armoury and prisons

TIP

- Winter visitors should dress warmly as there is no heating and it can be very cold.

Italy has a host of beautiful Gothic buildings, but the Palazzo Ducale is by far the most captivating: the seat of the doge and home to Venice's various offices of state for almost a thousand years.

Evolution The first ducal palace, completed in 814, was a severe fortress built on one of the few clay redoubts in the lagoon. This burned down in 976, as did its successor in 1106. By 1419 the palace was in its third—and final—incarnation. Three years later, the great hall, or Sala del Maggior Consiglio, was completed—one of many additions made to the interior. By 1550 most work had been completed, only to be undone by fires in 1574 and 1577, conflagrations that not only destroyed master-pieces by some of Venice's greatest painters,

Clockwise from far left: The Scala d'Oro (gold staircase) in the palazzo; a statue at the top of Scala dei Giganti; Ponte dei Sospiri (Bridge of Sighs); the astrological clock in the Sala Senato; a view along the outside of the building

but also threatened the entire building with collapse. Restoration work continued on and off until the 1880s.

Details Outside, note the famous Ponte dei Sospiri (Bridge of Sighs), tucked down a canal at the palace's eastern end, and the fine corner sculptures. Don't miss the excellent carving of the pillars and capitals, and the palace's superb main doorway, the Porta della Carta (1438–43), with the famous little knights, or tetrarchs, to its left. An ornate staircase leads up several flights to the beginning of a marked route leading from one lavishly decorated room to the next. Look for works by Tintoretto, Veronese and other Venetian masters. Tintoretto's gargantuan *Paradiso* (1588–92), the world's largest oil painting, is in the Sala del Maggior Consiglio.

THE BASICS

www.museiciviciveneziani.it

🔢 J6

✉ Piazzetta San Marco, San Marco 30124

☎ Palace and booking for guided tours 041 271 5911 or 041 520 9070

🕐 Palace Apr–Oct daily 9–7; Nov–Mar 8.30–5.30. Ticket office closes 1 hour earlier

🍴 Palace café

🚤 All services to San Zaccaria, San Marco Vallaresso or San Marco Giardinetti

♿ Poor: steps to upstairs

💰 Expensive (joint Piazza San Marco ticket)

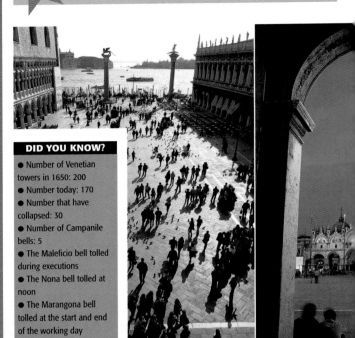

DID YOU KNOW?

- Number of Venetian towers in 1650: 200
- Number today: 170
- Number that have collapsed: 30
- Number of Campanile bells: 5
- The Maleficio bell tolled during executions
- The Nona bell tolled at noon
- The Marangona bell tolled at the start and end of the working day
- All bells tolled at the election of a pope or doge
- Prisoners were hung in cages from the Campanile
- Elevator added in 1962

HIGHLIGHTS

Avoid visiting Piazza San Marco on your first morning as the crowds might turn you against Venice. When you do visit, arrive early to beat the crowds to see the basilica, Palazzo Ducale and Campanile.

Hordes Europe's 'drawing room' was how Napoleon described Venice's main square, though glancing at today's crowds he would probably be less complimentary. Arrive early or in the evening, however—or off-season— and the piazza can still work its considerable charms. Over and above the obvious sights and (expensive) cafés, make a point of taking in the Zecca (mint), the Procuratie (administrative offices), the underrated Museo Civico Correr, and the Libreria Sansoviniana, considered one of the greatest buildings of its

Far left: Looking down on to Piazza San Marco; middle: The view through an arch to Basilica di San Marco and the Campanile; below: From the Campanile there is a good view towards the island of Murano

day. Also see the Torre dell'Orologio (▷ 75) and notice the two granite columns on the waterfront besides the Palazzo Ducale.

Campanile Take the tiny elevator up the basilica's detached bell tower for the views, which can stretch as far as the Alps. The original campanile, which at 98.5m (323ft) was the city's tallest building, dated from the 11th century. Erosion and shallow foundations (20m/66ft deep) proved the tower's undoing and, on 14 July 1902, it collapsed, though there were no casualties. It was rebuilt, as the Venetians insisted, *dov'era e com'era*—'where it was and how it was'—and opened on 25 April 1912, exactly 1,000 years after its predecessor. This time, though, it was 650 tons lighter and supported by an extra 1,000 foundation piles.

HIGHLIGHTS

● The main exhibition hall and stairway
● The view over the Basin of St. Mark from the Punta della Dogana
● The Torrino

TIPS

● Allow time to enjoy the building as well as the art.
● There's an excellent bookshop and pleasant café/bar within the complex.

Venice's most exciting contemporary space, wonderfully positioned where the Canal Grande opens into St. Mark's Basin, show-cases cutting-edge, 21st-century art in a converted 17th-century building.

The history The buildings of the Dogana di Mare, Venice's historic customs house, stand at the tip of Dorsoduro, the Punta della Dogana, where the Giudecca Canal merges with the Canal Grande. These warehouses, culminating in a tower and portico, were designed by Giuseppe Benoni and built between 1677 and 1682. Neglected for years, in 2007 the buildings were leased by the city to François Pinhault, owner of the Palazzo Grassi (▷ 70). In June 2009, after a €20 million restoration, the 3,440sq m (37,000sq ft) space opened as

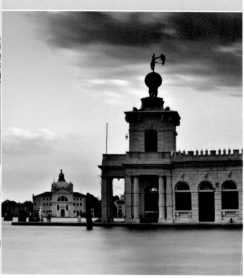

Far left: Maurizio Cattelan's Untitled 2007; *middle: the* Boy with a Frog *sculpture by Charles Ray stands outside the galleries and alongside the Canal Grande; below: Punta della Dogana at dusk*

a permanent contemporary art museum, its interior transformed by Japanese minimalist architect Tadao Ando. Inspired by traditional vernacular architecture, the interior fuses the old brick and stone with steel, glass and concrete.

The galleries Pinhault's personal vision and taste dictate much of what's on show—an evolving display that he views as an ongoing project, featuring works from his collection as well as commissioned pieces from up-and-coming artists. Among the former, work by Richard Prince, Rachel Whiteread, Jeff Koons, Cindy Sherman and Jake and Dinos Chapman have been on show. The violence inherent in some contemporary work is disturbing, but the Punta della Dogana has brought a new vibrancy to the Venetian art scene.

THE BASICS

www.palazzograssi.it

☩ H7

✉ Campo di Salute, Dorsoduro 2

☎ 041 523 1680

🕐 Daily 10–7

🍴 Museum café serving snacks and light meals

🚤 Salute

♿ Good

💰 Expensive

HIGHLIGHTS

● The Ponte di Rialto
● The Pescheria
● The produce stalls

TIP

● Remember the fish market is closed on Monday and there are no markets on Sunday.

The Ponte di Rialto, one of Venice's most iconic sights, spans the Canal Grande to link the *sestiere* of San Marco with the Rialto, once the city's commercial hub and still home to the main food markets.

The Ponte di Rialto The *rivo alto*, the 'high bank', was one of the firmest areas of the lagoon, so it's no surprise that the first settlements of Venice grew up here, the district becoming the commercial heart of the city. The two banks were linked by a pontoon bridge and the first permanent wooden structure went up in the 13th century. Merchants traded European goods with exotic imports from the East, while international banks and trading companies influenced prices across the known world. This monopoly ceased in 1498, when

Clockwise from far left: The beautiful Ponte di Rialto; a stall in the fish market on the Rialto; looking across the bridge towards Campo San Bartolomeo; the bridge lit at night

Vasco da Gama rounded the Cape and opened up sea routes to India and the Far East. The present bridge (1588–91) was designed by Antonio da Ponte, who won the commission in a competition, beating architects Palladio and Sansovino. The shops are later additions.

The markets The Rialto is still a trading centre, though today the accent is on food, with the open areas crammed with fish, fruit and vegetable stalls. The surrounding streets, whose evocative names recall the commodities traded here, house some of the city's best grocers, butchers, bakers, dairy shops and delicatessens. There's no better way to appreciate Venice as a living city than to join the morning shoppers and enjoy the sights, scents and sounds of one of Europe's most colourful markets.

THE BASICS

- H4/5
- Ponte di Rialto
- Market Mon–Sat 8–12.30; fish market closed Mon
- Bars in and around the food markets
- Rialto Mercato 1, Rialto 1, 2
- Poor
- Free

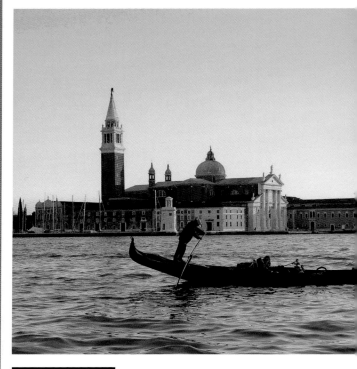

HIGHLIGHTS

- Facade (1559–80)
- Lighthouses (1828)
- Campanile (1791)
- *Adoration of the Shepherds*, Jacopo Bassano
- *The Fall of Manna*, Tintoretto
- *The Last Supper*, Tintoretto
- Choir
- View from the campanile

The view from the Campanile di San Marco is spellbinding, but if asked their best viewpoint many Venetians would probably nominate the bell tower of San Giorgio Maggiore, a magnificent Palladian church near the Giudecca.

Classical The church's dazzling marble facade provides one of the great panoramic set pieces of the Venetian skyline. Founded in 790, the first church on the site was destroyed by an earthquake in 1223, together with an adjoining Benedictine monastery built in 982. While the monastery was rebuilt in 1443, the church had to wait until 1559 and the arrival of the great Vicenzan architect, Andrea Palladio. His design for the new church adopted many of the architectural idioms of the ancient world

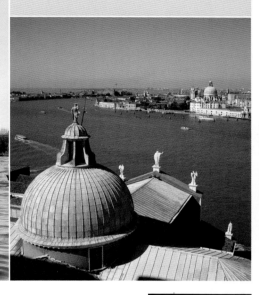

Left: A gondola passes in front of the cathedral of San Giorgio Maggiore, with its bell tower to the left of the picture; below: The view from the bell tower across the lagoon

(notably the majestic four-column portico) to produce one of Italy's most beautiful neoclassical buildings.

Interior The ancient world also influenced the sparse interior, where light is introduced by high windows, a device borrowed from the bath-houses of third-century Rome. The major works of art are Jacopo Bassano's *Adoration of the Shepherds* (1582), above the second altar on the right, and a pair of outstanding paintings by Tintoretto—*The Fall of Manna* (1594) and *The Last Supper* (1594)—on the walls of the chancel. Behind the high altar is the choir (1594–98), with its impressive wooden stalls, and down a corridor off the north aisle is the elevator up the campanile. The trip to San Giorgio is worth it for the views alone.

THE BASICS

➕ K8
✉ Campo San Giorgio, Isola di San Giorgio Maggiore
☎ 041 522 7827
🕐 Daily 9.30–12.30, 2.30–4.30 (6.30 May–Sep). Times can vary (particularly in winter)
🍽 Giudecca
🚢 San Giorgio N, 2
♿ Poor
💶 Campanile moderate

PAVLO CALIARIO VERONEN PICTORI
NAT° Æ. AMVLO ARTIS MIRACVLO
SV ERST YE FAT S FAMA VICTVRO

HIGHLIGHTS

- Sacristy
- Ceiling
- Choir and Nuns' choir
- Organ
- *St. Nicholas* (1563), Titian (first chapel on right)
- *Madonna and Child* (16th century), Tommaso Lombardo (second chapel on right)
- *Tomb of Archbishop Podocattaro of Cyprus* (d.1555), Sansovino (fourth chapel on right)

While paintings by some of Venice's artists—notably Titian and Tintoretto—are often showcased in grandiose settings, the city's finest collection of works by Veronese is in the humble little church of San Sebastiano.

Veronese Born in Verona, Paolo Caliari Veronese (1528–88) moved to Venice while he was in his twenties, settling close to San Sebastiano, which became his parish church. In 1555 he was commissioned to decorate the sacristy, where he left paintings of the *Evangelists* and the *Coronation of the Virgin*. Impressed by his work, the church authorities gave him free rein to decorate the ceiling. The three main panels depict episodes from the story of Esther, chosen for its symbolic parallels with the stories of Eve and the Virgin Mary.

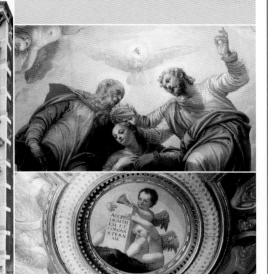

Clockwise from far left: A statue of Veronese in the church; the facade of San Sebastiano; detail of the *Coronation of the Virgin* by Veronese, which decorates the sacristy; *Cherubi*, also by Veronese, is part of the decoration on the ceiling

Monopoly Veronese also painted the high altarpiece—the *Madonna and Child with Saints Sebastian, Peter, Francis and Catherine* (1570)—and the two vast paintings on the north and south walls. The latter portray *Saints Mark and Marcellinus Led to Martyrdom and Comforted by St. Sebastian* and *The Second Martyrdom of St. Sebastian* (Sebastian survived his first assault by arrows and was martyred by being pummelled to death). Veronese also painted *The Trial and Martyrdom of St. Sebastian* in the nuns' choir, above the church's west end. He even designed and painted the organ.

His decorative monopoly of San Sebastiano makes it only fitting that he was buried here. His tomb, and that of his brother, lie in front of the chapel.

THE BASICS

www.chorusvenezia.org
🔢 D7
✉ Campo San Sebastiano, Dorsoduro 1686
☎ 041 275 0462
🕐 Mon–Sat 10–5, Sun 1–5
🍴 Campo Santa Margherita and Campo San Barnaba
🚤 San Basilio N, 2, 61, 62
♿ Good
💶 Inexpensive
❓ Chorus Pass (▷ 4)

HIGHLIGHTS

- Facade bas-reliefs (1440), Antonio Gambello
- Upper facade, Mauro Coducci
- *Madonna and Child with Saints*, Giovanni Bellini
- Relics of San Zaccaria
- *The Birth of John the Baptist*, Tintoretto
- Crypt
- Vault frescoes, Andrea del Castagno
- Altarpieces, Antonio Vivarini and Giovanni d'Alemagna
- Predella, Paolo Veneziano

San Zaccaria is a charming medley of Gothic and Renaissance architecture. Its calm interior contains Giovanni Bellini's *Madonna and Child with Saints*, one of Venice's most beautiful altarpieces.

Changes San Zaccaria was founded in the ninth century, received a Romanesque veneer a century later, and was overhauled once more in 1174. Rebuilding began again in the 14th century, when the church acquired a Gothic look, though no sooner had it been completed than another new church was begun. Old and new versions are still visible, the brick facade of the earlier church on the right, the white marble front of the latter to its left. The newer facade is one of the most important in Venice, displaying a moment of architectural

Clockwise from far left: The restored Madonna and Child with Saints by Giovanni Bellini (1505); the church was built in the 15th century and completed by Mauro Coducci; the bell tower; the lower facade is Gothic and the upper part Renaissance in style; marble carvings on the ceiling

transition from Gothic to Renaissance. The Gothic lower half is by Antonio Gambello, while the Renaissance upper section (added after Gambello's death in 1481) is the work of Mauro Coducci.

Who's who? The nave's second altar contains Giovanni Bellini's *Madonna and Child with Saints* (1505). Across the nave in the second altar on the right lie the relics of San Zaccaria (Zachary), father of John the Baptist. The 'museum' off the south aisle has linked chapels; the first has an early Tintoretto, *The Birth of John the Baptist*. The vaults of the adjoining Cappella di San Tarasio have early Renaissance frescoes by Andrea del Castagno and Gothic altarpieces by Antonio Vivarini. Steps lead to a ninth-century crypt, resting place of eight doges.

THE BASICS

➕ K6
✉ Campo di San Zaccaria, Castello 4693
☎ 041 522 1257
🕐 Mon–Sat 10–12, 4–6, Sun 4–6
🍴 Campo San Provolo
🚤 All services to San Zaccaria
♿ Good
💶 Church free. Cappella di San Tarasio inexpensive

HIGHLIGHTS

- Facades
- Martial bas-reliefs
- Plaque recording 1916 incendiary bomb
- Campanile's stone mask
- Interior
- *Madonna della Misericordia*, Bartolomeo Vivarini
- *Santa Barbara*, Palma il Vecchio

Santa Maria Formosa's appeal rests partly in its surrounding square. An archetypal Venetian *campo*, it is a pleasantly rambling affair, full of local vibrancy and lined with attractive cafés and palaces.

The structure This church takes its name from *una Madonna formosa*, 'a buxom Madonna', which appeared to St. Magnus in the seventh century, instructing him to follow a small white cloud and build a church wherever it settled. The present building, completed in 1492, was grafted onto an 11th-century Byzantine church, from which it borrowed its Greek-cross plan, a common feature of Byzantine (and later) churches dedicated to the Virgin. The facade (1542) was paid for by the Cappello family, hence its statue of Vincenzo Cappello,

Left: Santa Barbara by Palma il Vecchio depicts her flanked by other saints; below: Santa Maria Formosa was built onto an earlier Byzantine church

a Venetian admiral. Note the carved face on the bell tower to the left, one of Venice's most famous grotesques.

Interior The church's interior is a unique blend of Renaissance decoration and ersatz Byzantine cupolas, barrel vaults and narrow-columned screens. Of particular interest are two paintings, the first being Bartolomeo Vivarini's *Madonna della Misericordia* (1473), a triptych in the first chapel on the right (south) side. It was financed by the church's congregation which is depicted in the picture sheltering beneath the Virgin's protective cloak. The second, and more famous picture, Palma il Vecchio's *Santa Barbara* (1522–24), depicts the patron saint of artillerymen, and portrays the artist's daughter as its model.

THE BASICS

www.chorusvenezia.org

➕ J5

✉ Campo Santa Maria Formosa, Castello 5263

☎ 041 275 0462

🕐 Mon–Sat 10–5, Sun 1–5

🍴 Campo Santa Maria Formosa

🚤 Rialto or Fondamente Nove N, 1, 2, 4, 41, 42, 51, 52

♿ Good

💶 Inexpensive

❓ Chorus Pass (▷ 4)

TOP 25

HIGHLIGHTS

● *Madonna and Child*, Giovanni Bellini
● *Assumption*, Titian
● *Madonna di Ca' Pesaro*, Titian
● *Madonna and Child* (1339), Paolo Veneziano (sacristy)
● *St. John the Baptist*, Donatello
● *Mausoleo Tiziano* (Tomb of Titian)
● Wooden choir (124 stalls)
● *Monumento al Doge Giovanni Pesaro*
● *Monumento al Canova*

If you were allowed to walk away with just one work of art from Venice it could well be Bellini's sublime altarpiece in this church, the largest and most important in the city.

Magnificent edifice The Frari narrowly outranks Santi Giovanni e Paolo in size and importance. Founded around 1250, it became the mother church of the city's Franciscans, after whom it is named—*frari* is a Venetian corruption of *frati*, meaning 'friars'.

The greats interred Many of the city's great and good are buried in the church, among them the painter Titian (d.1576), whose 19th-century tomb occupies the second altar on the right (south) wall. Opposite, on the left wall, stands the *Monumento al Canova*

Far top left: A triptych (1488) by Giovanni Bellini, depicting the Madonna and Child with saints and angels; far bottom left: The tomb of Doge Francesco Dandelo; middle: Carved wooden inlaid stalls in the Gothic-Renaissance choir; below: A statue of Jacopo Negretti

(1827), an unmistakable marble pyramid that contains the sculptor's heart. The composer Claudio Monteverdi (d.1643) is buried in the third chapel to the left of the high altar.

Art Titian's compelling and stylistically innovative *Assumption* (1516–18) above the high altar immediately draws your eye, and don't miss the same artist's influential *Madonna di Ca' Pesaro* (1526), near the north door. The church's most beautiful painting, however, is Giovanni Bellini's sublime triptych of the *Madonna and Child between Sts. Nicholas, Peter, Mark and Benedict* (1488), in the sacristy. In the first chapel on the right of the high altar is Donatello's statue of *St. John the Baptist* (1438), the only work in Venice by the famous Florentine sculptor.

THE BASICS

www.basilicadeifrari.it
🔢 E5
✉ Campo dei Frari 3072, San Polo 3072
☎ 041 275 0462
🕐 Mon–Sat 9–6, Sun 1–6. Last admittance 5.30
🍴 Campo dei Frari
🚢 San Tomà N, 1, 2
♿ Good: one or two steps
💶 Inexpensive
❓ Chorus Pass (▷ 4)

HIGHLIGHTS

- Tinted marbles
- Decorative inlays
- False pillars
- Bas-reliefs
- Nuns' choir
- Balustrade
- Pillar carving
- Raised choir
- *Madonna and Child*, Nicolò de Pietro
- Ceiling

You'll soon get used to being brought up short in Venice by surprises and views around almost every corner, but none of them quite compares with your first glimpse of the beautiful marbles of Santa Maria dei Miracoli.

Miracles The church was built to house an image of the Virgin, painted in 1409 and originally intended to be placed on the outside of a house (a common practice in Venice). Miracles *(miracoli)* began to be associated with the image in 1480, leading to a flood of votive donations that enabled the authorities to commission a church for the icon from Pietro Lombardo. One of the leading architects of his day, Lombardo created a building that relied for its effect almost entirely on shades,

Left: The unusual interior makes use of marble and is decorated with statues by the architect Pietro Lombardo and his sons; below: Lombardo also used marble to great effect on the exterior of the church

hues and tints, facing his church in a variety of honey-toned marbles, porphyry panels and serpentine inlays.

Interior grandeur Lombardo's innovative use of marble continues on the inside, which is filled with an array of sculptures that were executed in tandem with his sons, Tullio and Antonio. The best include the carving on the two pillars that support the nuns' choir (near the entrance); on the half-figures of the balustrade fronting the raised choir; and among the exotica at the base of the choir's pillars. The striking ceiling portrays *50 Saints and Prophets* (1528), by Pier Pennacchi and his assistants. Nicolò di Pietro's *Madonna and Child*, the miraculous image for which the church was built, adorns the high altar.

THE BASICS

www.chorusvenezia.it

➕ J4

✉ Campo dei Miracoli, Cannaregio 6075

☎ 041 275 0462

🕐 Mon–Sat 10–5, Sun 1–5

🍴 Campo Santa Maria Nova

🚤 Rialto N, 1, 2, 4

♿ Good

💰 Inexpensive

❓ Chorus Pass (▷ 4)

HIGHLIGHTS

● Marble floor
● *Descent of the Holy Spirit*, Titian
● *The Virgin Casting out the Plague*, Juste le Court
● *Feast at Cana* (1561), Tintoretto (sacristy)
● *Cain and Abel* (1542–44), Titian (sacristy)
● *David and Goliath* (1542–44), Titian (sacristy)
● *Sacrifice of Abraham* (1542–44), Titian (sacristy)
● *St. Mark Enthroned between Sts. Cosmas, Damian, Roch and Sebastian* (1510), Titian (sacristy)

In a city where almost every street and canal offers a memorable vista, this church, proudly situated at the entrance to the Canal Grande, forms part of the famous panorama most people commonly associate with Venice.

Plague In 1630 Venice found itself ravaged by a plague so severe that the Senate promised to build a church in celebration of the Virgin if she could save the city. Within weeks the pestilence had abated and, on 1 April the following year, the first stone of the Salute, meaning 'health' and 'salvation' in Italian, was laid. Its architect was Baldassare Longhena. His design proved to be a baroque model for years to come, combining the Palladian influence of his master, Vincenzo

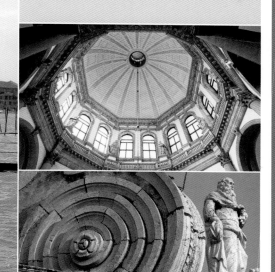

Clockwise from far left: Santa Maria della Salute has been listed as a World Heritage Site by UNESCO; the church seen from gondolas and other passenger craft; the interior of the dome; a view of a circular detail and statue on the exterior

Scamozzi (Andrea Palladio's closest follower), with a range of personal innovations.

Baroque interior The Salute's main impact is as a distant prospect, its dazzling exterior detail and great dome (fashioned on that of St. Peter's in Rome) forming irreplaceable elements of the Venetian skyline. The church's interior is more restrained, and its fine marble floor first catches the eye. Moving left from the side entrance, the third of the three altars boasts an early work by Titian, the *Descent of the Holy Spirit* (1550). The high altar supports *The Virgin Casting out the Plague* (1670), a magnificent sculpture designed by Longhena and carved by Juste le Court. The supplicant figure represents Venice, while the elderly harridan moving off right symbolizes the plague.

THE BASICS

+ G7
✉ Campo della Salute, Dorsoduro
☎ 041 522 5558
🕐 Daily 9–12, 3–5.30
🚤 Salute 1
♿ Poor: several steps
🎫 Church free. Sacristy inexpensive

HIGHLIGHTS

● Main portal
● *Monument to Doge Pietro Mocenigo*, Pietro Lombardo
● *St. Vincent Ferrer*, Giovanni Bellini
● *St. Antonius Pierozzi Giving Alms to the Poor*, Lorenzo Lotto
● *Monument to Doge Michele Morosini*
● Veronese ceiling paintings, Cappella del Rosario
● Capella della Madonna della Pace

Nowhere in Venice is there a greater collection of superb sculpture under one roof than in this majestic Gothic church. The walls here are lined with the funerary monuments of more than 20 of the city's important doges.

Monuments Santi Giovanni e Paolo, known locally as San Zanipolo, is rivalled only by Santa Maria Gloriosa dei Frari (▷ 48–49). Its appeal rests on a handful of superb paintings, its tremendous tombs, and on surroundings that include the magnificent facade of the adjacent Scuola Grande di San Marco and Verrocchio's great equestrian statue of Bartolomeo Colleoni. The church was begun in 1246 by Doge Giacomo Tiepolo, who is buried in the most ornate of the four wall tombs built into the

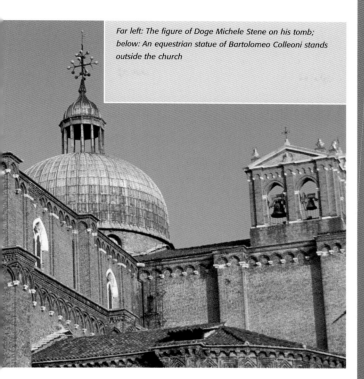

Far left: The figure of Doge Michele Stene on his tomb; below: An equestrian statue of Bartolomeo Colleoni stands outside the church

facade. Inside, further tombs lie around the walls, many by some of Venice's finest medieval sculptors. The best include the monuments to Doge Pietro Mocenigo (d.1476) by Pietro, Tullio and Antonio Lombardo (left of the main door), and to Doge Michele Morosini (d.1382), on the wall to the right of the high altar.

Paintings The most outstanding of the church's paintings are Giovanni Bellini's beautiful and recently restored polyptych of St. Vincent Ferrer (1464, second altar on the right) and the works in the south transept, which include *The Coronation of the Virgin*, attributed to Cima da Conegliano, and Lorenzo Lotto's wonderful *St. Antonius Pierozzi Giving Alms to the Poor* (1542).

THE BASICS

- J4
- ✉ Campo Santi Giovanni e Paolo, Castello 6363
- ☎ 041 523 7510
- 🕐 Mon–Sat 9–6.30, Sun 3–6.30
- 🍽 Campo Santi Giovanni e Paolo
- 🚢 Fondamente Nove or Ospedale 41, 42, 51, 52
- ♿ Good: one step
- 💶 Inexpensive

HIGHLIGHTS

- Facade
- Stucco staircase
- Ceiling paintings
- Albergo and Archivio
- *Judith and Holofernes*, Piazzetta
- *St. Nicholas of Bari*, Lorenzo Lotto
- *Nativity*, Cima da Conegliano

Giovanni Battista Tiepolo's paintings are not to all tastes, but those in the intimate Scuola Grande dei Carmini, all pastel shades and fleshy figures, are a change from the drama of Titian or Tintoretto.

Carmelites The Carmelite Order's Venetian chapter was originally installed in Santa Maria del Carmelo (or Carmini), the Carmelite church just to the left of the *scuola* (▷ right). In 1667 the order commissioned Baldassare Longhena to design a new home in the present building (Longhena also designed Santa Maria della Salute and a number of palaces on the Canal Grande).

Exuberant ceilings The highlights are Giovanni Battista Tiepolo's nine ceiling paintings

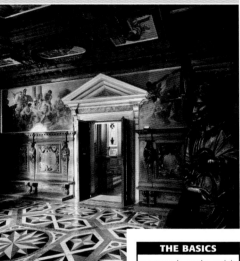

(1739–44) in the Salone. The paintings' central panel depicts the vision of St. Simon Stock, elected the Carmelites' prior-general in 1247, in which the Virgin appears to the saint with a 'scapular'. This garment of two linked pieces of cloth became central to Carmelite belief as wearers were promised relief from the pains of purgatory on the 'first Sunday after death'. Two adjacent rooms, the Albergo and Archivio, have heavy wooden ceilings and several paintings, the best of which is Piazzetta's *Judith and Holofernes* (1743).

Chiesa dei Carmini Be sure to visit the church to see Lorenzo Lotto's *St. Nicholas of Bari* (1529), by the side door (second chapel), and Cima da Conegliano's fine *Nativity* (1509) above the second altar on the (south) wall.

THE BASICS

www.scuolagrandecarmini.it

✚ D6

✉ Campo dei Carmini, Campo Santa Margherita, Dorsoduro 2617

☎ 041 528 9420; church 041 296 0630

🕐 Daily 11–4

🍴 Campo Santa Margherita

⛴ Ca' Rezzonico 1

♿ Poor: stairs to main rooms

💶 Moderate

Chiesa dei Carmini

🕐 Mon–Sat 2.30–5.30

💶 Free

HIGHLIGHTS

● *Crucifixion*
● *Moses Strikes Water from the Rock*
● *The Fall of Manna*
● *The Temptation of Christ*
● *The Adoration of the Shepherds*
● *Wooden sculptures*
● *The Flight into Egypt*
● *Annunciation*

TIPS

● Allow 1 to 2 hours for a thorough visit.
● Start your visit upstairs in the Albergo.

In a city of superlative and striking works of art, there can be few that make such a marked and powerful first impression as the colossal cycle of 54 paintings by Tintoretto that line the walls here.

From rags to riches This *scuola*, formerly a charitable institution for the sick, was founded in 1478 in praise of St. Roch, whose efficacy against disease made him popular in pestilence-ridden Venice. In 1564, as one of wealthiest fraternities, the *scuola* instigated a competition to decorate its hall. The winner, Tintoretto, spent some 23 years creating one of Europe's greatest painting cycles.

The wonders inside To see Tintoretto's 54 paintings in the order they were painted, ignore

TOP 25

the canvases on the ground level and in the main hall (Sala Grande) up the stairs. Instead, go to the Sala dell'Albergo (off the main hall), dominated by a huge *Crucifixion* (1565), often described as one of Italy's greatest paintings. The room's central ceiling panel is *St. Roch in Glory*, the painting that won Tintoretto his commission. In the main hall are ceiling paintings (1575–81) describing episodes from the Old Testament, all carefully chosen to draw parallels with the *scuola*'s charitable or curative aims. The 10 wall paintings show scenes from the New Testament. Note the superb 17th-century wooden carvings around the walls, by the little-known sculptor Francesco Pianta. Of the eight paintings downstairs, the artist's last in the *scuola* (1583–88), the best are the idiosyncratic *Annunciation* and *The Flight into Egypt*.

THE BASICS

www.scuolagrande
sanrocco.it

➕ E5

✉ Campo San Rocco, San Polo 3052

☎ 041 523 4864

🕐 Daily 9.30–5.30

🍴 Campo dei Frari

🚏 San Tomà N, 1, 2

♿ Poor

💷 Expensive

❓ A leaflet about the *scuola*'s paintings is usually free with your ticket

59

Scuola di San Giorgio degli Schiavoni

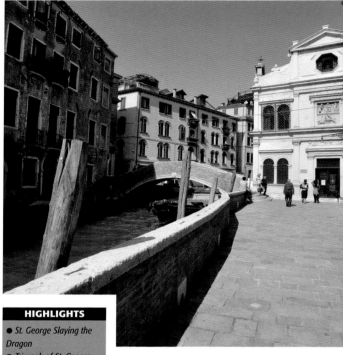

HIGHLIGHTS

● *St. George Slaying the Dragon*
● *Triumph of St. George*
● *St. George Baptizing the Gentiles*
● *The Miracle of St. Tryphon*
● *The Agony in the Garden*
● *The Calling of St. Matthew*
● *The Vision of St. Augustine*

TIP

● Allow time for your eyes to accustom to the dim light, and take time to pick out the detail in the paintings.

This intimate *scuola,* with its charming Carpaccio paintings, allows you the opportunity to look at works of art in the building for which they were painted, rather than in a gallery venue.

Slavs This tiny *scuola* (religious or charitable confraternity) was founded in 1451 to look after Venice's Dalmatian, or Slav *(Schiavoni),* population. Dalmatia, roughly present-day Croatia, was among the first territories absorbed by Venice (in the ninth century). In 1502 Carpaccio was commissioned to decorate their humble *scuola* with scenes from the lives of Dalmatia's three patron saints: George, Tryphon and Jerome. On their completion (in 1508), the paintings were installed in the headquarters' upper gallery

Clockwise from left: Looking towards the scuola; detail of St. George Slaying the Dragon by Carpaccio; stone fish detail on the exterior

and moved to their present position when the *scuola* was rebuilt in 1551.

Art cycle The nine-painting cycle starts on the north wall with the wonderfully graphic *St. George Slaying the Dragon* (1502–08), while to its right is the *Triumph of St. George*, *St. George Baptizing the Gentiles* and *The Miracle of St. Tryphon*, which depicts the obscure boy-saint exorcizing a demon from the Roman Emperor's daughter. Right of the altarpiece by Carpaccio's son, Benedetto, are *The Agony in the Garden* and *The Calling of St. Matthew*, followed by three works featuring St. Jerome, an early church father. The best known is the *Vision of St. Augustine*, with the saint in his study having a vision announcing Jerome's death.

THE BASICS

➕ K5

✉ Calle dei Furlani, Castello 3259/a

☎ 041 522 8828

🕐 Mon 2.45–6, Tue–Sat 9.15–1, 2.45–6, Sun 9.15–1

🍴 Fondamenta di San Lorenzo

🚤 All services to San Zaccaria

♿ Good

🎫 Moderate

HIGHLIGHTS

● Basilica di Santa Maria Assunta
● Santa Fosca church
● View from the campanile

The evocative rural backwater of Torcello, dreaming in the past, is Venice's most ancient settlement and the site of a superb basilica, the oldest building in the lagoon.

Seeing Torcello From the landing stage a path runs beside Torcello's canal, crossed by the simple stone span of the Ponte del Diavolo (Devil's Bridge), to the main piazza. Around here everything there is to see is grouped. You will also find the so-called Trono di Attila, a primitive stone chair once used by the bishop.

Island churches One of the most magical places in Venice, Torcello was probably the city's birthplace and the first area of the lagoon settled in the fifth century. Malaria and the silting up of its canals snuffed out its prosperity

Clockwise from far left: The view from the bell tower across Torcello; candles inside Santa Fosca church; Madonna and child mosaic in Santa Maria Assunta; exterior of Santa Fosca; a canal runs through farmland; a mosaic depicting hell in Santa Maria Assunta

in the 12th century, and today it is home to little more than a single hamlet and a beautiful patchwork of green fields and leafy canals. Torcello is dominated by the cathedral of Santa Maria Assunta. This is Venice's oldest building (founded 639) and one of its loveliest sights as well as the finest Veneto-Byzantine church in Italy. The lofty interior, bare and cool, has some superb mosaics dating from the ninth to 12th centuries, on the vaults and walls. Climb the bell tower for wonderful lagoon views across the mudflats and marsh. Also worth seeing close by are the 11th-century Byzantine church of Santa Fosca and the small Museo dell'Estuario, which houses a low-key display of archaeological finds from Torcello and the lagoon. The perfect antidote to the crowds and heat of Venice.

THE BASICS

✚ Off map to northeast
🚢 LN from Fondamente Nove to Burano then the 'T' boat to Torcello, every 60–90 min; takes 45 min. Get the earliest boat to avoid a crowd

Museo dell'Estuario
☎ 041 250 1780
🕐 Mar–Oct daily 10.30–5.30; Nov–Feb 10–5
💷 Inexpensive

Basilica di Santa Maria Assunta
☎ 041 296 0630
🕐 Mar–Oct daily 10.30–6; Nov–Mar 10–5
❓ Bell tower temporarily closed
💷 Church and bell tower inexpensive. Moderate for combined ticket

MORE TO SEE

More to See

This section contains other great places to visit if you have more time. Some are in the heart of the city while others are a short journey away, found under Further Afield. This chapter also has fantastic excursions that you should set aside a whole day to visit.

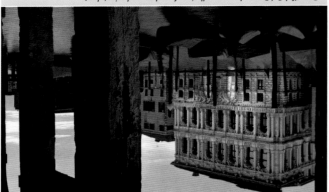

Beautiful Ca' Pesaro houses galleries of modern and oriental art

In the Heart of the City

ANGELO RAFFAELE

The ancient church of the Archangel Raphael was founded in the eighth century; the present Greek cross-shaped building, with its two bell towers, dates from the 17th. Well off the beaten track, its visitor numbers soared following the success of Salley Vickers' book *Miss Garnet's Angel*; the church plays a starring role in the novel. Above the main door stands a charming statue of the Angel, holding the hand of the boy Tobias, accompanied by a dog, and holding a fish, which plays a key role in the story. Inside, there are more reminders of the apocryphal story, with the stars of the show painted on the organ loft by Gianantonio Guardi.

➕ C6 ✉ Campo Angelo Raffaele, Dorsoduro 1710 🕐 Daily 9–12, 3–5 🚤 San Basilio 2, 8 💶 Free

ARSENALE

The Arsenale, Venice's vast former shipyards, are now used for exhibitions during Venice's *Biennale* and for the annual

Festival of Boats each May. Work on opening more areas, more frequently, is ongoing with a view to reinstating the entire area as a vibrant part of the city.

➕ L6 ✉ Campiello della Malvasia, Castello ☎ 041 270 9546 🚤 41, 42, 71, 72 💶 Varies with exhibition

CA' PESARO

www.museiciviciveneziani.it

The Ca' Pesaro presents its best face to the Canal Grande, but its waterfront facade can also be glimpsed from the ends of several alleys off the Strada Nova. It was bought as three separate buildings in 1628 by the Pesaro family, who subsequently commissioned Baldassare Longhena, one of Venice's leading 17th-century architects, to unite the component parts behind one of the city's grandest baroque facades. Today it houses Venice's Galleria d'Arte, Galleria Internazionale d'Arte Moderna (Gallery of Modern Art) and the Museo d'Arte Orientale displaying Chinese and Japanese art and objects.

CAMPO DEI MORI

⊞ G4 ⊠ Canal Grande-Fondamenta Ca'
Pesaro, Santa Croce 2070-76 ☎ 041 544
0662 ⊙ Galleria and Museo Apr–Oct Tue–
Sun 10–6; Nov–Mar 10–5 ⊠ San Stae N, 1
⬥ Poor 💰 Galleria and Museo moderate

This sleepy little square may take
its name either from the Moorish
merchants who traded on the
fondaco nearby, or from three silk
merchants—Robia, Sandi and Alfani
Mastelli who settled in the Palazzo
Mastelli north of the *campo*. In
time they may have inspired the
so-called *Mori* (Moors), three
statues built into the walls of the
piazza's houses. The building
stands just east of the square at
No. 3399 and was home to the
painter Tintoretto between 1574
and his death in 1594.
⊞ C2 ⊠ Campo dei Mori, Cannaregio
🚊 Orto 41, 42, 51, 52

CAMPO SANTA MARGHERITA

This may well become your
favourite Venetian square, thanks
mainly to its friendly and informal
air, its collection of little bars and
cafés, and its easy-going street life,
which remind you that Venice is
still—just—a living city. It's busy
with Venetians throughout the day,
shopping at the market stalls in the
morning, meeting to chat and sip
coffee in the afternoon while
children play and dogs race round.
Evenings see flocks of students
from the nearby university drinking
outside bars; Margaret Duchamp,
on the corner, il Caffè and il Doge
are all popular and have outside
tables. The Scuola Grande di San
Rocco (▷ 58), the Frari (▷ 48),
and the Accademia (▷ 24) are
within easy reach.
⊞ E6 ⊠ Dorsoduro 🍴 Cafés 🚊 Ca'
Rezzonico 1

GESUITI

This lofty, shadowy and incredibly
ornate church, built by the Jesuits
in 1715, is renowned for its
extraordinary marble *trompe-l'oeil*,
best seen in the pulpit on the left,
whose solid stone is carved to
resemble pelmets, tassels and
curtains of figured damask and
velvet. The church also boasts

Informal Campo Santa Margherita

Tintoretto's house in Campo dei Mori

Titian's *Martyrdom of St. Lawrence* (in the first chapel on the left) and Tintoretto's *Assumption of the Virgin* (in the left transept).

➕ J3 ✉ Campo dei Gesuiti, Cannaregio 4885 ☎ 041 528 6579 🕐 Daily 10–12, 4–6/7 ♿ Good 🚤 Fondamente Nove 41, 42, 51, 52 💰 Free

IL GHETTO

The Venetian ghetto lies in a fascinating area half-hidden in a corner of Cannaregio, enclosed by canals. The city's Jewish population were forced to live here until 1527. The district, which gave its name to all similar enclaves, most likely took its name from the foundries where cannon were cast (*gettare* means to cast). The area is still one rich in Jewish culture and history, including a monument to the city's Jews murdered during the Holocaust, synagogues and the Jewish museum, the Museo Ebraico.

➕ E2

Museum

✉ Campo Ghetto Nuovo, Cannaregio 2902 ☎ 041 715 359; www.museoebraico.it 🕐 Sun–Fri 10–6 (7 in summer) 🚤 Guglie

Colourful apartment buildings in Il Ghetto

Tulips blooming in Giardini ex Reali

GIARDINI EX REALI

About the only patch of green in the vicinity of Piazza San Marco is the Giardini ex Reali, a waterfront oasis of trees behind the Procuratie Nuove. Benches are shaded by trees and the view over the Bacino di San Marco is superb, but the downsides are the constant crowds and the tightly packed rows of souvenir stalls.

➕ H6–J6 ✉ San Marco 🚤 San Marco Vallaresso, San Marco Giardinetti N, 1, 2 💰 Free

GIARDINO PAPADOPOLI

An oasis of green, the Giardino Papadopoli, once one of the largest private gardens in Venice, stands at the west end of the Grand Canal, a stone's throw from bustling Piazzale Roma. It's a great place to wait for transportation to the mainland, by road or rail—you can reach the station across the Ponte della Costituzione, opened in 2007 to mark the new

41, 42, 51, 52 or San Marcuola N, 1, 2 💰 Moderate

millennium. The gardens were laid out in 1810 when a group of buildings were demolished, including the church of Santa Croce, which gave its name to this *sestiere*.

➕ D4 ✉ Fondamenta Papadopoli 🚤 Piazzale Roma 1, 2 🎟 Free

ISOLA DI SAN MICHELE

It's a short hop on the *vaporetto* to Venice's atmospheric cemetery island with its Renaissance church. Most of Isola di San Michele is covered by the cemetery, where Venetians are buried in tiers of stone coffin drawers or rest under an assortment of monuments. Don't miss the tombs of the composer Stravinsky and the impresario Serge Diaghilev.

➕ L1–L2 ✉ Isola di San Michele ☎ 041 729 2811 🕐 Apr–Sep daily 7.30–6; Oct–Mar 7.30–4; 25 Dec, 1 Jan 7.30–12 🚤 Cimitero 🎟 Free

MERCERIE

The *calli* between San Marco and Rialto are known as the Mercerie, once synonymous with luxury goods. Today, the shops sell everything from expensive high fashion to tourist kitsch.

➕ H5 🚤 Rialto N, 1, 2, 4

MUSEO DELLA FONDAZIONE QUERINI STAMPALIA

www.querinistampalia.it

The Fondazione Querini Stampalia, housed in a Renaissance *palazzo*, promotes study and culture. Its modernized ground floor is a excellent example of the work of architect Carlo Scarpa. The museum is in the unchanged period rooms on the second floor, giving a real taste of an 18th-century *palazzo*. Stars of the show are Giovanni Bellini's superb *Presentation in the Temple* and two series of paintings: 67 studies of Venetian festivals by the 18th-century artist Gabriele Bella, and a collection of genre paintings by Pietro Longhi (1702–85) showing everyday Venetian life.

➕ J5 ✉ Campiello Querini Stampalia, Castello 5252 ☎ 041 271 1411 🕐 Tue–Sun 10–7 🚤 San Zaccaria, 1, 2, 42, 52 🎟 Expensive

MORE TO SEE

The cemetery on Isola di San Michele

The Geography Lesson *by Pietro Longhi in Museo della Fondazione Querini Stampalia*

MUSEO STORICO NAVALE

If you expected a dull and perfunctory museum, the Museo Storico Navale is a revelation. Its enjoyably presented displays of maritime ephemera put Venice and the sea into a clear historical context.

➕ M7 ✉ Campo San Biagio, Castello 2148 ☎ 041 520 0276 🕐 Mon–Fri 8.45–1.30, Sat 8.45–1 🚢 Arsenale 1, 41, 42 ♿ Poor 💷 Inexpensive

PALAZZO CONTARINI DEL BOVOLO

www.scalabovolo.org

This Gothic *palazzo* is best known for its sinuous exterior staircase. Such staircases are called *scale a chiocciola* (snail stairs) in Italian—the Venetian dialect for snail is *bovolo*. The beautiful redbrick and Istrian stone stairway gives access on five levels to graceful loggias curving around inside a tower.

➕ G6 ✉ Calle dei Risi, San Marco ☎ 041 270 2464 🚢 Rialto N, 1, 2

PALAZZO GRASSI

www.palazzograssi.it

Outside, nothing could be more traditionally 18th-century classical than this palace. Inside, it's another story; the interior was converted in the 1980s by Gianni Agnelli of Fiat to become Venice's most high-profile exhibition venue. In 2004, following the death of Agnelli, it was bought by François Pinault, the French millionaire collector and owner of a business empire that includes Gucci. It reopened in 2007 as a venue for temporary exhibitions, designed to be seen in conjunction with the collection at the Punta della Dogana (▷ 36–37) and centred round Pinhault's own collection of more than 2,000 pieces of 20th- and 21st-century contemporary art.

➕ F6 ✉ Campo San Samuele, San Marco 3231 ☎ 199 139 139 (in Italy), 00 39 0445 230313 (from abroad) 🕐 Wed–Mon 10–7 🚢 1 Sant'Angelo, 2 San Samuele 💷 Expensive

PALAZZO MOCENIGO

www.museicivicveneziani.it

The Palazzo Mocenigo near San Stae is one of several *palazzi* in the city built by the Mocenigo

Museo Storico Navale

Palazzo Contarini del Bovolo with its famous exerior staircase

family, one of the grandest and oldest of the noble Venetian clans. The palace now houses the Museo del Tessuto e Costume and is worth a visit for a fascinating glimpse of the style in which the 18th-century nobility lived.

�� F4 ✉ Salizzada San Stae, Santa Croce 1992 ☎ 041 721 798 ⏰ Tue–Sun 10–4 🚤 San Stae N, 1 💷 Moderate

PONTE DELL'ACCADEMIA

All the bridges across the Canal Grande have mesmerizing views, but none perhaps as lovely as those looking east from the Ponte dell'Accademia. There's been a bridge here since 1854; today's is the third version. It's identical in design to the Ponte degli Scalzi at the station, but built of wood, as stone was too expensive for construction across this much wider stretch of water.

🔛 F7 ✉ Canal Grande 🚤 Accademia N, 1, 2, 4 ♿ Poor

RIVA DEGLI SCHIAVONI

This broad quayside with its procession of *palazzi*, historic hotels, stalls and cafés, has great views, and is an ideal place for an evening stroll.

🔛 K6–L6 ✉ Riva degli Schiavoni, San Marco to Castello 🚤 All services to San Zaccaria

SAN FRANCESCO DELLA VIGNA

San Francesco takes its name from a vineyard left to the Franciscans here in 1253. Many alterations have been made since, not least the facade, built by Palladio between 1562 and 1572. The best paintings are Antonio da Negroponte's *Madonna and Child* (1450), in the right transept, and Giovanni Bellini's *Madonna and Child* in the Cappella Santa, from where you can access the peaceful cloisters.

🔛 L5 ✉ Campo San Francesco, Castello 2786 ☎ 041 520 6102 ⏰ Daily 8–12, 3–7 🚤 Celestia 41, 42, 51, 52 ♿ Good 💷 Free

SAN GIACOMO DELL'ORIO

Few Venetian buildings feel as old as San Giacomo, founded in

Riva degli Schiavoni

Interior decoration at San Francesco della Vigna

the ninth century and added to over the years to produce an architectural hybrid. The 14th-century Gothic ship's-keel ceiling and the wooden Tuscan statue of the *Madonna and Child* are wonderful. There are magnificient paintings in the old and new sacristies and a high altarpiece, *Madonna and Child*, by Lorenzo Lotto.

🔲 F4 ✉ Campo San Giacomo dell'Orio, Santa Croce 1456 ☎ 041 275 0462; www.chorusvenezia.it 🕐 Mon–Sat 10–5, Sun 1–5 🚤 Riva di Biasio or San Stae 1 ♿ Good 🎟 Inexpensive ❓ Chorus Pass (▷ 4)

SAN GIOVANNI IN BRAGORA
Many people have a soft spot for San Giovanni in Bragora, the baptismal church of the Venetian composer Antonio Vivaldi.

Founded in the eighth century, San Giovanni in Bragora is one of Venice's oldest churches, its name deriving possibly from *brágora*, meaning 'market-place'; or from two dialect words, *brago* ('mud') and *gora* ('stagnant canal'); or

from the Greek *agora*, meaning 'town square'; from *bragolare* ('to fish'); or from the region in the Middle East that yielded the relics of St. John the Baptist, to whom the church is dedicated. The Venetian composer Antonio Vivaldi was baptized here, and the original font, together with copies of his baptismal documents, are in the left nave.

The paintings in the lovely interior begin on the south wall to the left of the first chapel with a triptych by Francesco Bissolo and a *Madonna and Saints* by Bartolomeo Vivarini. Between these, above the confessional, stands a small Byzantine Madonna. A relief above the sacristy door is flanked on the left by Alvise Vivarini's *Risen Christ* (1498) and by Cima da Conegliano's *Constantine and St. Helena* (1502). Cima also painted the church's pictorial highlight, *The Baptism of Christ* (1494). On the wall of the left aisle is a small *Head of the Saviour* by Alvise Vivarini and Bartolomeo Vivarini's

The attractive interior of the church of San Giovanni in Bragora

MORE TO SEE

Virgin Mary between John the Baptist and St. Andrew (1478), to the right of the second chapel.

➕ L6 ✉ Campo Bandiera e Moro, Castello 3790 ☎ 041 296 0630 🕐 Mon–Sat 9–12 🚤 Campo Bandiera e Moro 🚢 All services to San Zaccaria 🚶 Good 🎟 Free

SAN MAURIZIO

Rebuilt in the early 19th century and hardly used in the 20th, the church of San Maurizio found a new role in 2004 when it opened as a Vivaldi exhibition area. The chief draw is the fine collection of old musical instruments, whose sound provides the music that's a constant backdrop to your visit. You can buy CDs, tapes and DVDs relating to the composer.

➕ G6 ✉ Campo San Maurizio, San Marco ☎ 041 241 1840 🕐 Varies with exhibition 🎟 Free 🚢 Giglio 1

SAN NICOLÒ DEI MENDICOLI

San Nicolò was built in the 12th century and since 1966 has been restored by the Venice in Peril Fund. The interior is superbly decorated with marbles, statues, paintings and gilded woodwork.

➕ C6 ✉ Campo San Nicolò dei Mendicoli, Dorsoduro 1907 ☎ 041 270 2464 🕐 Mon–Sat 10–12, 4–6 🚢 San Basilio N, 2, 61, 62 🚶 Good 🎟 Free

SAN PANTALEONE

San Pantaleone is best known for its gargantuan ceiling painting, Gian Antonio Fumiani's *The Miracles and Martyrdom of St. Pantaleone* (1704). Smaller paintings include Veronese's touching piece *St. Pantaleone Healing a Boy* (1587; second chapel on the right).

➕ E5 ✉ Campo San Pantalon, San Polo 3765 ☎ 041 270 2464 🕐 Mon–Sat 3–6 🚢 San Tomà 1, 2 🚶 Good 🎟 Free

SAN POLO

Founded in 837 but much altered since, the church of San Polo is renowned for Giandomenico Tiepolo's *Via Crucis*, or *Stations of the Cross* (1747), an 18-panel cycle of paintings in the sacristy. Tintoretto's turbulent *Last Supper* (1547) hangs on the west wall, while the apse chapel contains

The view along a street to San Pantaleone

An exhibition in San Maurizio

Veronese's *Marriage of the Virgin*.
🞢 F5 ✉ Campo San Polo, San Polo 2102
☎ 041 523 7631 or 041 275 0462;
www.chorusvenezia.it 🕐 Mon–Sat 10–5,
Sun 1–5 🚢 San Silvestro 1 ♿ Good
🎟 Inexpensive ❓ Chorus Pass (▷ 4)

SANTO STEFANO

Delight in the sensation of walking from the heat and bustle of a city into a building that induces immediate calm, an effect gained by the soothing Gothic interior of this, one of Venice's loveliest churches. Ideally placed Santo Stefano sits on the edge of Campo Santo Stefano (also known as Campo Francesco Morosini), one of Venice's most charming squares; the nearby Paolin (▷ 150) is an ideal place to sit with a drink or ice cream.

The church has not always been so peaceful, having been reconsecrated six times to wash away the stain of blood spilled by murders within its walls. Today, its interior is overarched by an exquisite 'ship's keel' ceiling and framed by tie beams and pillars of Greek and red Veronese marble. In the middle of the nave lies Doge Francesco Morosini (d.1612, and buried under Venice's largest tomb slab), famous for recapturing the Peloponnese and blowing up the Parthenon with a single shot.

Other tombs command attention, notably Pietro Lombardo's *Monument to Giacomo Surian* (d.1493) on the wall to the right of the main door, but the church's chief artistic interest lies in the gloomy sacristy at the end of the right nave. The altar wall displays two narrow-framed Saints by Bartolomeo Vivarini, as well as a recessed 13th-century Byzantine icon. On the walls to either side are four paintings by Tintoretto and four portraits of Augustinian cardinals, displayed here as Santo Stefano is an Augustinian church.
🞢 G6 ✉ Campo Santo Stefano (Campo Francesco Morosini) Castello 2774
☎ 041 275 0462; www.chorusvenezia.it
🕐 Mon–Sat 10–5, Sun 1–5 🍴 Campo Santo Stefano 🚢 San Samuele or Sant' Angelo N, 1, 2, 4 ♿ Very good
🎟 Inexpensive ❓ Chorus Pass (▷ 4)

The leaning bell tower of Santo Stefano is a tourist attraction

SQUERO DI SAN TROVASO

Venice had more than 10,000 gondolas in the 16th century; today there are only a few hundred, built in a handful of specialist boatyards *(squeri)*. One of the most famous, and easiest to see, is the Squero di San Trovaso, on the waterfront of the Rio San Trovaso, just behind the Zattere. Construction sheds and workshops are set back from the *rio*, and there's generally activity of some sort as gondolas are repaired. Modern water conditions take a toll on the boats, which suffer from the backwash of motorboats, and they need to be cleaned and overhauled as often as once a month. To get a real insight into the expertise of the gondolier, take a *traghetto* across the Canal Grande and watch the oarsmen.

➕ E7　✉ Rio San Trovaso, Dorsoduro　🚤 Zattere N, 2, 51, 52, 61, 62

TEATRO LA FENICE

www.teatrolafenice.it

Fenice is the Italian word for phoenix, and Venice's opera house, designed by Giannantonio Selva in 1792, rose from the ashes of the disastrous fire of 1996 to reopen for the 2004–5 season. The new hall is a delight. Book well in advance for performances or join one of the regular tours.

➕ G6　✉ Campo San Fantin, San Marco 1965　☎ 041 786 611　🕐 Daily with audio guides to fit around rehearsals; check with theatre. For group guided tours tel 041 24 24; www.hellovenezia.com　🚤 Giglio 1　💰 Expensive

TORRE DELL'OROLOGIO

San Marco's clock tower was built between 1496 and 1506. The exterior stone dial shows the 24 hours in Roman numerals; the interior face shows the signs of the zodiac and phases of the moon.

➕ J6　✉ Piazza San Marco, San Marco 30124　☎ 848 082 000 (from abroad 00 39 041 427 3089); online reservations at www.vivsticket.it (reservations compulsory)　🕐 Guided visits in English Mon–Wed 10, 11, 1, Thu–Sun 2, 3, 5　💰 Expensive (with Piazza San Marco joint ticket)　🚤 San Marco Vallaresso, San Marco Giardinetti N, 1, 2 and all services to San Zaccaria

The auditorium, Teatro La Fenice

Torre dell'Orologio has been restored

Further Afield

BURANO

In the Museo del Merletto are breathtaking, intricate examples of traditional lace. The island's fame in part rests on its many brightly painted houses, whose wonderful bold colours make its streets and canals as picturesque as Venice itself. Fishing boats moor at the island's fringes and nets are laid out to dry by the road, and despite the faint air of commercialism and the many visitors, it feels like a genuine fishing community.

➕ a4–c5 ✉ Isola di Burano 🚢 LN (Laguna Nord) from Fondamente Nove, every 60–90 min

Museo del Merletto

➕ b5 ✉ Piazza Galuppi 187 ☎ 041 730 034 🕐 Apr–Oct daily 10–6; Nov–Mar 10–5 💷 Moderate

THE LIDO

The Lido is essentially a long, narrow sandbank, once a sparsely inhabited island of dunes and pine-woods. Today it combines its role as a residential suburb with that of a seaside resort and overspill hotel area for Venice. A 10-minute boat trip from the city will bring you to a different world, where cars, buses and supermarkets are the backdrop to lazy beach days. More active pursuits include tennis and golf, as well as walking and cycling.

➕ Off map to southeast ℹ Gran Viale Santa Maria Elisabetta 6a, Lido di Venezia ☎ 041 526 5721 🕐 Jun–Sep daily 9–12.30, 3.30–6 🚢 Lido

SANT'ERASMO

Bigger than Venice itself, Sant'Erasmo is one of the lagoon's best-kept secrets. It lies northeast of the city, a long, flat, sparsely inhabited island where sandy paths crisscross well-kept fields and tiny vineyards. Sant'Erasmo produces huge quantities of vegetables for the city markets. The island is traversed by a single road, where rickety old unlicensed cars trundle up and down. The island does have a tiny store at the main settlement, built around the church, and a couple of *trattorie*.

➕ Off map to northeast ✉ Isola di Sant' Erasmo 🚢 Capannone, Chiesa, Punta Vela 13 from Fondamente Nove a Murano

A quiet canal at dawn with moored vessels and colourful houses

Excursions

CHIOGGIA

www.turismovenezia.it/chioggia

This excursion takes in the west end of the Lido and the island of Pellestrina en route to the ancient town of Chioggia.

Pellestrina is a contrast to the developed, bustling Lido, a sand-swept spit of land, bordered on the sea side by the *murazzi*, the sea defence walls erected in the 18th century. Its three main villages earn their living from fishing, both from the boats you'll see moored and from the floating huts just offshore.

Chioggia is a Roman foundation and one of the earliest settlements on the lagoon, a past reflected in its layout, a grid pattern of three straight streets intersected by canals. The main street, Corso del Popolo, is lined with old buildings and is home to the 14th-century *granaio* (grainstore), behind which is the *pescheria*, the fish market. Further along the Corso are the churches of Sant'Andrea Apostolo, San Jacopo and the Duomo (cathedral).

Past here, the Museo Civico della Laguna Sud is housed in a 15th-century Franciscan convent. It tells the story of Chioggia and the southern lagoon, with displays on the Roman epoch and a collection of boats and fish-ing artefacts on the upper floors.

From here, head east along the main Canale della Vena, an almost impossibly picturesque waterway with brightly painted fishing boats, tiny arcaded shops, fruit and vegetable stalls and flapping washing in the adjoining court-yards. The waterfront is the main food shopping street and thronged all morning, while the narrow *calli* leading off illustrate how the town has retained its medieval layout.

The church of San Domenico, standing on its own island at the lagoon end, was founded in the 13th century and contains the 1520 *St. Paul,* the last picture painted by Carpaccio.

Do try to include lunch while in Chioggia; the restaurants here are noted for their fish and seafood, and prices are lower than in Venice. You could stop on the way back to town for a swim at one of the Lido beaches.

Distance: From the Lido 25km (16 miles)
Journey time: 1 hour from the Lido
Transport: Co-ordinated bus and waterbus service; No. 11 bus from Lido, connect with *motonave* 11 to Chioggia from Pellestrina

Musei Civico della Laguna del Sud

✉ San Francesco Fuori le Mure, Campo Marconi, Chioggia ☎ 041 550 0911
🕐 12 Jun–Aug Tue–Wed 9–1, Thu–Sat 9–1, 7.30–11.30, Sun 7.30pm –11.30pm; Sep–11 Jun Tue–Wed 9–1, Thu–Sat 9–1, 3–6, Sun 3–6 💰 Moderate

Bridge over the Canale della Vena

PADUA

www.turismopadova.it

Historic Padua is a university city and important economic centre, where art, monuments, churches and excellent shops scatter a compact, attractive centre. Aim to arrive early, taking the tram from outside the station to the centre.

The historic hub centres around the Palazzo della Ragione, medieval Padua's assembly hall and law courts, built 1218–19. The vast building has a remarkable cycle of 15th-century astrological frescoes in the main hall, which also contains a huge wooden horse, constructed for a tournament in 1466. The ground floor has been home to food stalls for more than 800 years, while the Piazza della Frutta and Piazza dell'Erbe, on each side of the *palazzo*, host one of northern Italy's most vibrant produce markets.

Near here is the splendidly eclectic Caffè Pedrocchi, whose upstairs rooms, the 19th-century centre of Padovan intellectual life, are decorated in every style from Egyptian and Etruscan to Renaissance. South of here, reached down Via del Santo, is the Basilica di Sant'Antonio, one of Italy's main pilgrim shrines, built between the mid-13th and 14th centuries and flanked by a superb equestrian bronze of Gattamelata by Donatello (1453).

Padua's main artistic site lies to the north, nearer the station, a complex including the Cappella degli Scrovegni, the Musei Civici Eremitani and the Palazzo Zuckermann. The Scrovegni chapel was built in 1300 by Enrico Scrovegni to atone for his father's usury. From 1303 to1309 the walls were frescoed by Giotto with scenes from the life of Christ and the Virgin, set against a radiant blue background. Considered one of the turning points in Western art, the perspectival elements, the realistic details and expressions show a wholly innovative naturalism and fluency. The other parts of the complex showcase archaeology, sculpture, painting and the decorative and applied fine arts.

A statue outside Basilica San Giustina

Distance: 32km (20 miles)
Journey time: 25–35 min
Transport: Bologna line from Venezia Santa Lucia; GSITA buses from Piazzale Roma
🛈 Stazione FS ☎ 049 875 2077
🕐 Mon–Sat 9.15–7, Sun 9–12
🛈 Galleria Pedrocchi ☎ 049 876 797
🕐 Mon–Sat 9–1.30, 3–7

Cappella degli Scrovegni

www.cappelladegliscrovegni.it
✉ Piazza Eremitani 8 ☎ 049 201 0020; book 72 hours in advance, tickets to be collected 1 hour in advance 🕐 Daily 9–7
💷 Expensive

VICENZA

www.vicenzae.org

Cradled in green hills, beautiful Vicenza, with its glossy shops, smart restaurants and easy life-style, is famed for its *palazzi* and civic buildings, the work of the 16th-century's most influential architect, the great Andrea Palladio.

Dating from Roman times, the town stands on two rivers and became a Venetian possession in 1404. Its architectural makeover came in the 16th century when Palladio and his neoclassical style burst upon the scene. Born in Padua, Palladio found his major patron, the humanist Trissino, in Vicenza and, between 1540 and 1580, transformed the city.

Vicenza is bisected by the Corso Palladio, lined with a procession of mansions and *palazzi*, no less than five designed by Palladio, while others are scattered throughout the city centre. The Corso opens into Piazza Matteotti, home to both the Teatro Olimpico and the Palazzo Chiericati (1550), one of Palladio's most triumphant buildings, now housing the Museo Civico and its fine art collection. Teatro Olimpico, Europe's oldest indoor theatre, was designed by Palladio in 1579 and opened in 1585. The architect died before it was complete, though the astonishing *trompe l'oeil* permanent stage set of a classical city was inspired by his designs.

South from here lies the Piazza dei Signori, the heart of the *centro storico*. The square is dominated by Palladio's Basilica, enclosing the earlier Gothic Palazzo della Ragione, and his Loggia del Capitaniato, flanked by the Monte di Pietà, Vicenza's 16th-century pawn shop.

Elsewhere you'll find the Palazzo Leoni Montanari, home to another museum, the Duomo (cathedral) and some interesting churches.

Outside Vicenza are two renowned Palladian villas, Villa Valmarana, nicknamed 'Ai Nani' after the stone dwarfs on its wall, with superb frescoes by Tiepolo father and son, and Villa Capra Valmarana, or Rotonda (1567).

Distance: 74km (47 miles)
Journey time: 55 min
Transport: Trains from Venezia Santa Lucia
🚹 Piazza dei Signori 8 ☎ 0444 544 122
🕐 Daily 10–2, 2.30–6.30

Teatro Olimpico

✉ Piazza Matteotti 11, 36100 Vicenza
☎ 0444 222 800 🕐 Sep–Jun Tue–Sun 9–5; Jul–Aug 9–7 💶 Expensive (combined ticket for all Vicenza sites)

Museo Civico–Pinacoteca

✉ Palazzo Chiericati, Piazza Matteotti 37–39
☎ 0444 222 811 🕐 Sep–Jun Tue–Sun 9–5; Jul–Aug 10–6 💶 Expensive (combined ticket)

An ariel view across Vicenza

City Tours

This section contains self-guided tours that will help you explore the sights in each of the city's regions. Each tour is designed to take one or two days, with a map pinpointing the recommended places along the way. There is a quick reference guide at the end of each tour, listing everything you need in that region, so you know exactly what's close by.

CITY TOURS

San Marco

The historic *sestiere* of San Marco, the true heart of the city, is packed with *palazzi,* churches, museums, shops and restaurants. It runs east of the Canal Grande, from the iconic Piazza San Marco west towards the Rialto and its famous bridge.

Morning
Start your day in the **Piazza San Marco** (▷ 34–35; right), visiting the rich interior of the basilica before the hordes of day-visitors from the cruise boats and coaches arrive. Then take the elevator up the **Campanile** (▷ 34–35), from where you'll get a bird's-eye view of the city, its lagoon and the islands, the perfect way to get your Venetian bearings.

Mid-morning
Splash out on mid-morning coffee at one of the piazza's celebrated cafés, before you stroll across to the **Palazzo Ducale** (▷ 32–33). Here, in the vast and opulent chambers, you'll get an insight into the grandeur and riches of Venice at the height of its power. If you want to learn more, spend an hour in the **Museo Civico Correr** (▷ 30–31) at the opposite end of the piazza.

Lunch
There's a huge choice of lunch possibilities between the piazza and the **Rialto** (▷ 38–39)—a good bet would be **Acquapazza** (▷ 144), where you can sit outside and enjoy the freshest of fish on Campo Sant'Angelo, one of the area's nicest *campi.*

Afternoon
Spend the afternoon wandering through the maze of streets and squares towards the Rialto and its bridge, perhaps visiting the **Teatro La Fenice** (▷ 75), taking in some contemporary art at **Palazzo Grassi** (▷ 70; left), or the lovely **Santo Stefano** (▷ 74). If you're flagging, use the *vaporetti* along the Canal Grande.

CITY TOURS

Mid-afternoon

It's time to browse the shops of San Marco, where you'll find everything from the cheapest souvenirs to serious *alta moda* (high fashion). Good areas to shop are along the **Mercerie** (▷ 69), around Campo San Bartolomeo at the **Rialto** (▷ 38–39; right), or go where the serious money spends its cash and head for Calle Vallaresso, around the church of San Moïse and along the Largo XXII Marzo, an area that's home to just about every top Italian designer you can name. If souvenir stalls are your thing, take in the waterfront by the **Giardini ex Reali** (▷ 68), where itinerant artists also sell their work.

Evening

Aim to finish your stroll on Campo Santo Stefano, where you can have a drink or one of the best ice creams in town at **Paolin** (▷ 150).

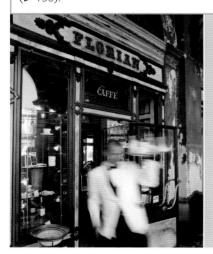

Dinner

Have dinner away from the piazza itself, but be sure to return later to see this wonderful space as it should be seen, thronged with people and buzzing with conversation; not for nothing did Napoleon call it the 'finest drawing room in Europe'. Pull up a chair, listen to the music and sip a final glass of Prosecco at **Florian** (▷ 147; left) or **Quadri**.

Ramo Cazza

C d Callion

San Giacomo dell'Orio
C Ilo d'Morti

C d Savio

C de Rioda

C de Rioda

Ruga Vecchia

Palazzo Mocenigo

Ruga Bella

Palazzo Corner della Regina

Casa Favretti

Santa Maria Mater Domini

Campo N Sauro

Agnus Dio

Palazzo Brandolin

C te dell' Anatomia

Campo San Giacomo dell'Orio

Palazzo Mariani

Palazzo Zane

San Cassiano

C lle di Cristo

Palazzo Grioni

Santa Maria Domini

Campo S Cassiano

Palazzo Moro

Palazzo Zane-Collalto

Campo d'Agostin

Palazzo Giustinian

Palazzo Gozzi

Palazzo Muti-Baglioni

Scuola Grande di San Giovanni Evangelista

Palazzo Molin

Palazzo Bernardo

Palazzo Albrizzi

C lle Albrizzi

Palazzo Molin-Cappella

San Giovanni Evangelista

Palazzo Donà delle Rose

SAN POLO

Archivio di Stato

Palazzo Corner Mocenigo

Palazzo Zen

Campo San Polo

Palazzo Soranzo

Sant' Aponal

San Rocco

Santa Maria Gloriosa dei Frari

San Polo

Palazzo Maffetti-Tiepolo

Campo S Silvestro

San Silvestro

Campo dei Frari

Salizz S Polo

Palazzo Barzizza

Palazzo Ravà

San Silves

Scuola Grande di San Rocco

Campo S Rocco

Palazzo Donà della Madonnetta

Palazzo Papadopoli

Palazzo Corner

Museo Casa Carlo Goldoni

Palazzo Corner

Palazzo Grimani

Palazzo Donà

Palazzo Bernardo

Palazzo Martinengo

Palazzo Signolo Loredan

Campo S Tomà

S Tomà

Palazzo Pisani-Moretta

Palazzo Barbarigo

Palazzo Cappello-Layard

Palazzo Contarini dei Cavalli

Palazzo Grimani

Palazzo Dolfin

Palazzo Tiepolo

Palazzo Benzon

San Benedetto

S L

Palazzo Persico

Palazzo Marcello dei Leoni

Sant'Angelo

Campo S Benedetto

Teatro Rossini

Palazzo Civran Grimani

Santa Tomà

Santa Tomà

Palazzo Corner-Spinelli

Palazzo Balbi

Palazzo Contarini delle Figure

Palazzo Mocenigo

Palazzo Curti

Museo Fortuny

Palazzo Da Lezze

Oratio dell'Annunziata Acquapazza

Are Ver

Ca' Foscari

Palazzo Giustinian

Palazzo Morolin

Campo S Angelo

Palazzo Nani

Palazzo Grassi

San Samuele

Campo S Samuele

Campiello Novo

Santo Stefano

Campiello Fenice

Ca' Rezzonico

San Barnaba

Contarini-Michiel

Ca' Rezzonico

Palazzo Malipiero

San Samuele

Paolin

Puntolaguna

San Maurizio

C lle Caleghen

Teatro La Fen

Palazzo Stern

Palazzo Moro

Ca' del Duca

Campo Santo Stefano

Palazzo Loredan

C d Cerchieri

Palazzo Falier

San Vidal

Campo Pisani

Santa Maria del Giglio

Bergama

Palazzo Loredan

Rio d Toletta

Palazzo Contarini degli Scrigni

Palazzo Giustinian Lolin

Campo S Vidal

Palazzo Morosini

Palazzo Bellavite

Palazzo Zaguri

C Ostreghe

Palazzo Malipiero

C d Toletta

Accademia

Palazzo Querini

Palazzo Franchetti

Palazzo Pisani

Campo S Maurizio

Palazzo Pisani Gritti

FMI

Pala

Palazzo Brandolin

Palazzo Giustinian Recanati

Campo d Carità

Ponte dell'Accademia

Palazzo Barbaro

Palazzo Barbarigo

Fond di Tranghetto

Pala Flang

San Trovaso

Campo S Trovaso

Gallerie dell'Accademia

Palazzo Contarini-Dal Zaffo

Palazzo Loredàn

Palazzo Corner (Ca' Grande)

S Maria del Giglio

Canal Grande

Santa Maria del Giglio

Palazzo Nani

Palazzo Cini

Campo S Vio

Collezione Peggy Guggenheim

Palazzo Salviati

Palazzo Dario

Ex Abbazia di San Gregorio

Squero di San Trovaso

S Maria d Visitazione

S Agnese

Campo S Agnese

Palazzo Da Mula

Fond Venier

Palazzo Barbaro

Palazzo Genovese

Ex Abbazia San Gregori

Ex Chiesa

Gesuati

Campo S Domenico

Ex Convento

Ex Ospizio

Zattere

Fond Zattere ai Gesuiti

Zattere

Ospedale degli Incurabili

Canale della Giudecca

Fond Zattere ai Catecumeni

E   F   G

Ca' d'Oro
Ca' d'OroFoscari
Palazzo
sagredo
S Sofia
Palazzo
S Sofia

Scuola
Michiel
delle Colonne
dell'Angelo
Custode

Santi
Apostoli

Campo
Santi Apostoli

Palazzo
Widman

Campiello
Widman

Cte d Paludo
Cte d Paludo

Palazzo
Widman

Pescheria
Campo
d Pescaria

Ca da
Mosto

Rio di Santa Apostoli

San Caciano
Cpl S
Crosette

San
Canzian
Campo
S Maria Nova

Ospedale
Civile

Fabbriche
Nuove

Ca da
Mosto

Palazzo
Bembo
e Boldù

Santa Maria
dei Miracoli

Scuola Grande
di San Marco

Fabbriche
Vecchie
Rialto
Mercato

Lion-Morosini
Rialto

Palazzo

San Giovanni
Crisostomo

Palazzo
Sanudo

Monumento
di Bartolomeo
Colleoni

Campo Santi
Giovanni
e Paolo

Gobbo

Teatro
Malibran

Palazzo
Dolfin

Santi Giovanni
e Paolo

Giovanni di Rialto
mosinario

S Giacomo
d Rialto

Erberia dei Tedeschi

Fondaco

Palazzo
Bragadin
Carabba

Palazzo
Pisani

Campo
Rialto
Nuovo

Palazzo
Dieci Savi

Rialto

Palazzo
Marcello

Ponte
di Rialto

Fondaco
dei
Tedeschi

San Lio

Palazzo
Dona

Rialto
Rialto

San Bartolomeo

Palazzo
Priuli

Palazzo
Cavagnis

Palazzo
Dolfin-Manin
Palazzo
Bembo

Scuola Grande
di San Teodoro

Santa Maria
della Fava

Campo
Santa Maria
Formosa

Teatro
Goldoni

San
Salvador

Palazzo
Faccanon

Santa Maria
Formosa
Tasca-Papafava

Palazzo
Grimani

Mercerie

Palazzo
Soranzo

Fondazione
Querini
Stampalia

Palazzo
Zorzi

San
Zulian

S Giovanni
in Oleo

SAN
MARCO

Palazzo
Contarini
del Bovolo

San
Gallo

Torre dell'
Orologio

Procuratie
Vecchie

Piazza
San Marco

Basilica di
San Marco

Museo Diocesano
d'Arte Sacra

S Fantin

Museo
Civico
Correr

Caffè
Quadri

Campanile

Palazzo
Ducale

Palazzo
Dandolo

Riva degli
Schiavoni

Caffè
Florian

Museo
Archeologico

PONTE
DEI SOSPIRI

Palazzo
Prigioni

Procuratie
Nuove

Palazzo
Reale

Libreria
Sansoviniana

Leone di
San Marco

PONTE
DELLA
PAGLIA

San Zaccaria
(Piazza San Marco)

Giardini
ex Reali

Piazzetta
San Marco

Zecca

S Teodoro

Ridotto

Capitaneria
di Porto

San Marco

Palazzo
Giustinian

San Marco
(Vallaresso)

Palazzo
Tiepolo

Palazzo
Treves Bonfili

Punta
della Dogana

Punta della Dogana

Santa Maria
della Salute

Seminario
Patriarcale

| 0 | | 300 m |
| 0 | | 300 yds |

Campo
S Giorgio

San Giorgio
Maggiore

H   J

San Marco Quick Reference Guide

 SIGHTS AND EXPERIENCES

CITY TOURS

Basilica di San Marco (▷ 14)

A superb 1,000-year-old church, rich in mosaics, whose architecture looks both to ancient Byzantium and medieval Europe. The treasures inside the building match its striking interior. The altar is encrusted with precious gems.

Museo Civico Correr (▷ 30)

Venice's city museum, telling the story of the historic Republic through sculpture, paintings, maps and artefacts. The paintings here represent Venice's finest artists. A hall is dedicated to sculptures by Antonio Canova.

Palazzo Ducale (▷ 32)

Once the seat of government and home to the Doge, this extraordinary palace is unique architecturally and artistically. Here you will find the largest oil painting in the world, by Tintoretto. The Bridge of Sighs is nearby.

Piazza San Marco and Campanile (▷ 34)

Venice's greatest square, lined with splendid buildings and arcades, is dominated by the detached Campanile with its views over the city and lagoon, and in fine weather to the Alps.

Rialto (▷ 38)

Once the commercial hub of the city, the Rialto bridge spans the Canal Grande attracting locals and tourists to browse its wonderfully colourful fresh produce markets. Nearby streets house food shops.

CITY TOURS

Cannaregio

Venice's northwest *sestiere*, Cannaregio, one of the earliest areas to be developed, was, before the causeway and railway were built, the original entrance to the city. Full of contrasts, it sprawls from the station to the Rialto along the Canal Grande, an area that's busy and still densely populated by local Venetians. To the north, things are quieter, and you'll find peaceful residential streets running between the wide *fondamente* (quaysides) that line a trio of parallel canals lying to the south of the open waters of the lagoon.

Morning

The **Canal Grande** (▷ 20–21) is at its most animated in the mornings, when it's bustling with *vaporetti*, delivery barges and flotillas of gondola tours. There are few better places to take in all this activity than from the portico of the upper floor of the **Ca' d'Oro** (▷ 16–17; right), so kick off your day by visiting this beautiful *palazzo* and its museum.

Mid-morning

You'll emerge to turn left on to the **Strada Nova**, a string of wide streets which connects the Rialto with the station and was created in the 19th century when numerous old houses were demolished. There's plenty of choice for a coffee break and the area is known for its good-value and wide range of shops. Turn right when you get to the Canale di Cannaregio and cut through to visit **Il Ghetto** (▷ 68). From here, head north, following the *fondamenta* along one of Cannaregio's wide canals.

Lunch

There's a choice of lunch spots along these canals; you could enjoy some *cichetti* (Venetian-style tapas) or a full lunch at **Anice Stellato** (▷ 145; left) or take your time at the **Osteria l'Orto dei Mori** (▷ 149–150).

Afternoon

After lunch, cut through the **Campo dei Mori** (▷ 67) to visit the lovely church of **Madonna dell' Orto** (▷ 26–27). Then either walk or hop on the *vaporetto* to the Fondamenta Nuove, to take in the over-the-top delights of the sumptuous church of the **Gesuiti** (▷ 67–68; right).

Mid-afternoon

Follow the maze of streets south to **Santa Maria dei Miracoli** (▷ 50–51; left), one of Venice's loveliest churches and a popular spot for weddings.

CITY TOURS

Evening

Enjoy a drink at an outside table, either in **Campo Santa Maria Nova**, right near the Miracoli and one of Venice's most under-rated squares, or at a café in **Santi Apostoli**, always busy with locals and visitors.

Dinner

This part of Cannaregio has a good choice of restaurants and you couldn't do better than head for **Vini da Gigio** (▷ 151), which belongs to an association of restaurants that prides itself on serving genuine Venetian cuisine, with the accent on seasonal, fresh, traditional dishes. If you're up for more action, you could round off the evening by dropping in to Venice's **Casino** (▷ 135), housed in the magnificent Palazzo Vendramin Calergi, right on the Canal Grande.

Canale delle Sacche

Canale delle Navi

Sant Alvise

Ex Ospedale Psichiatrico Umberto I

Rio d Riformati
Fond d Riformati

Le Cappuccine
Palazzo Grimani Mayer

Ospedale Fatebenefratelli

Rio di Sensa
Fond di Sensa

Sant'Alvise
Campo S Alvise
Convento

Palazzo Michiel

S Girolamo

Rio di San Girolamo
Fond d San Girolamo

Anice Stellato

Scuola dei Mercan

Fond di Sensa

Fond Madonna dell'Orto
Rio Madonna dell'Orto

CANNAREGIO

Campo S Leonardo
Rio di Misericordia

Fond di Mori

Palazzo Mastell

Campo dei Mori

IL GHETTO

Museo Ebraico

Osteria l'Orto dei Mori
Palazzo Longo

Casa Tintoretto

Tempio Israelitico

Palazzo Nani

Fond di Misericordia

Ex Convento dei Servi di Maria

Rio Terra Farsetti

C llo dell'Anconeta
Lombardo

Cappella del Volto Santo

Palazzo Savorgnan

Parco di Savorgnan

Palazzo Venier

PONTE D GUGLIE

Guglie

Palazzo Diedo

Campo S Marzia

Rio Terra S Leonardo

Rio Terra di Maddalena

Ex Chiesa di San Leonardo

Ex Scuola di Cristo

La Maddalena

S Fosc

Palazzo Labia

Palazzo Emo

San Marcuola

Palazzo Vendramin-Calergi (Casinò)

Palazzo Correr Contarini

Palazzo Soranzo

Palazzo Correr Contarini

Palazzo Gritti

San Marcuola

Palazzo Molin

San Geremia e Lucia

Palazzo Flangini

Riva de Biasio

Palazzo Marcello Toderini

Palazzo Giovanelli

Fondaco dei Turchi

Canal Grande

Palazzo Belloni Battagia

Palazzo Emo

Palazzo Barbarigo

Palazzo Corner

Palazzo Gidoni-Bembo

Casa Correr

Museo di Storia Naturale

Ca' Priuli-Bon

San Stae

Palazzo Zulian

Palazzo Gussoni-Grimani della Vida

Palazzo Gritti

Palazzo Donà-Balbi

San Giovanni Decollato

Palazzo Priuli-Stazio

Palazzo Ca' Tron

Campo S Stae

Palazzo Boldù

S Simeon Grande

Palazzo Foscarini-Giovanelli

Ca' Pesaro

Museo del Tessuto e del Costume Palazzo Mocenigo

Palazzo Corner della Regina

Palazzo Donà

Casa Favrett

San Giacomo dell'Orio

Palazzo Agnus Dio

Palazzo Soranzo Cappello

Ruga Vecchia

Ruga Bella

Campo San Giacomo dell'Orio

Santa Maria Mater Domini

Palazzo Mariani

Palazzo Zanes

Palazzo Moro

S M Mater Domini

San Cassiano

Palazzo Brandoli

Campo S Cassiano

Scuola Grande di San Giovanni Evangelista

Palazzo Grioni

Palazzo Gozzi

Palazzo Muti-Baglioni

Palazzo Zane-Collalto

San Giovanni Evangelista

Palazzo Giustinian

Palazzo Albrizzi

Palazzo Molin-Cappella

Archivio di Stato

Palazzo Molin

Palazzo Donà delle Rose

SAN POLO

Sant' Aponal

Campo S Aponal

Palazzo Corner Mocenigo

Palazzo Zen

Campo San Polo

Palazzo Soranzo

Palazzo Maffetti-Tiepolo

San Polo

S Silvest

0   300 m

0   300 yds

Madonna dell'Orto

Madonna dell'Orto

QUARTIERE GRIMANI

Casin degli Spiriti

Isola di San Michele →

Palazzo Minelli Spada

Fond Caseario Contarini

Palazzo Contarini dal Zaffo

Sacca della Misericordia

Marziale

Scuola Vecchia della Misericordia

S Maria Valverde

Palazzo Lezze

Scuola Nuova della Misericordia

Palazzo Molin

Ex Chiesa di Santa Caterina

Gesuiti

Palazzo Donà

Fondamente Nove

Palazzo Papafava

Oratorio dei Crociferi

Palazzo Zen

Palazzo ndramin

Ex Convento

alazzo ovanelli

Felice

Vini da Gigio

Palazzo Seriman

ampo Felice

Palazzo ontana

a' d'Oro

Ca' d'Oro

S Sofia

Palazzo Foscari

Palazzo Sagredo

campo S Sofia

Santi Apostoli

Palazzo Widman

Palazzo S Sofia Michiel delle Colonne

Scuola dell'Angelo Custode

Ca' da Mosto

San Canzian

Santa Maria dei Miracoli

Scuola Grande di San Marco

Pescheria

Fabbriche Nuove

Palazzo Lion-Morosini

San Giovanni Crisostomo

Palazzo Bembo e Boldù

Palazzo di Bartolomeo Sanudo

Monumento Colleoni

Campo Santi Giovanni e Paolo

Fabbriche Vecchie

Rialto Mercato

Teatro Malibran

Palazzo Dolfin

Palazzo Pisani

Santi Giovanni e Paolo

Gobbo

San Giovanni di Rialto Elemosinario

Palazzo Civran

S Giacomo di Rialto

Fondaco

Palazzo Bragadin Carabba

Palazzo Marcello

Erberia dei Tedeschi

Rialto

Palazzo Dieci Savi

Ponte di Rialto

Rialto

San Bartolomeo

San Lio

Palazzo Donà

Palazzo Priuli

SIGHTS AND EXPERIENCES

Ca' d'Oro (▷ 16)

The Ca' d'Oro, set right on the Canal Grande and one of Venice's finest Venetian-Byzantine *palazzi,* is a perfect example of a rich medieval merchant's home and place of business. It was built between 1420 and 1434 for the Contarini family and gets its name —the House of Gold—from the glittering decoration that once adorned the exterior. Today, it houses an eclectic museum.

Madonna dell'Orto (▷ 26)

This gem of a church, set in a quiet and undiscovered area on Venice's northern fringes, was founded in 1350 and rebuilt in the Gothic style between 1399 and 1473. The facade combines Gothic and Renaissance elements, while the interior is pure, airy Gothic. The superb paintings are almost all by Tintoretto, who lived nearby and is buried here. He created these works as a gift to the church.

Santa Maria dei Miracoli (▷ 50)

This perfectly proportioned and balanced Renaissance church, set alongside a canal, was built in the 1480s in honour of a miraculous shrine to the Virgin that stood nearby. The exterior is faced with polychrome marble panels, columns and pilasters, best admired from the bridge. Inside, the light-filled space has intricate and delicate carving and sculptures.

Restaurant tables set out in Campo Santa Maria Nova

Castello

Castello, the biggest Venetian *sestiere*, stretches from San Marco in the west to encompass the islands of San Pietro and Sant'Elena in the east. Historically, its shipbuilding Arsenale was the city's industrial heart, still surrounded by a vibrant working-class district. Its cityscape is varied, with a long southern waterfront, the Riva degli Schiavoni, overlooking St. Mark's Basin and a northern quayside that looks towards the main lagoon islands and the distant Alps.

Morning

Head first for **Campo Santa Maria Formosa**, where you can visit the church (▷ 46–47; right) and take in the art collection at the **Museo della Fondazione Querini Stampalia** (▷ 69) before exploring the surrounding *calli,* busy at this time of day with locals shopping. From here, head up to **Santi Giovanni e Paolo** (▷ 54–55) and its *campo*, now home to Venice's main hospital, housed behind the superb facade of what was once the Scuola Grande di San Marco.

Mid-morning

Emerging from the church, take a pause to enjoy a drink at one of the cafés surrounding the *campo*, before using your map to wend your way through the labyrinthine alleys to the serene Palladian church of **San Francesco della Vigna** (▷ 71). From here follow the crowds southeast towards the **Arsenale** (▷ 66), a short hop from the **Museo Storico Navale** (▷ 70) where you can learn more about Venice's maritime history.

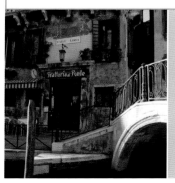

Lunch

There are plenty of lunch places here as you're back on the continuation of the **Riva degli Schiavoni** (▷ 71)—head for the good value places on Via Garibaldi or cut though to **Da Remigio** (▷ 147) for a quintessentially Venetian eating experience at this traditional restaurant.

Afternoon

Now is the time to take in the glowing pictures in the **Scuola di San Giorgio degli Schiavoni** (▷ 60–61), before heading west to contrast this with the artistic treasures in **San Zaccaria** (▷ 44–45).

Mid-afternoon

You could relax after this by taking the *vaporetto* to **Giardini**, an area of cool trees, benches and green open spaces, part of which is home to the permanent buildings used during Venice's annual Biennale art shows, showcasing art and architecture in alternate years.

CITY TOURS

Evening

Don't miss a pre-dinner drink on the waterfront (left), with views across St. Mark's Basin to the island of **San Giorgio Maggiore** (▷ 40–41).

Dinner

Castello has some of the best restaurants in Venice; try the old-established and renowned **Corte Sconta** (▷ 147; right), the superb **Osteria alle Testiere** (▷ 149) or the **Osteria Oliva Nera** (▷ 150), where you'll find the best of contemporary Venetian cooking.

3

Ex Convento

Calle larga dei Bottieri

Canale delle Fondamenta Nuove

Palazzo
Seriman

Rio delle Fondamenta Nuove

Santi
Apostoli

San Lazzaro
dei Mendicanti

Ospeda

Campo
Santi Apostoli

Palazzo
Widman

Ospedale
Civile

Santa Maria
del Pianto

San
Canzian

4

San
Selvatico

Scuola Grande
di San Marco

Palazzo
Lion-Morosini

Santa Maria
dei Miracoli

Monumento
di Bartolomeo
Colleoni

Campo Santi
Giovanni
e Paolo

Santi Giovanni
e Paolo

San Giovanni
Crisostomo

Palazzo
Civran

Teatro
Malibran

Fondaco
dei Tedeschi

Palazzo
Bragadin
Carabbà

Palazzo
Dolfin

Palazzo
Pisani

Ospedaletto
(Santa Maria
dei Derelitti)

Santa Maria
dei Derelitti

Barbaria delle Tole

San Lio

Palazzo
Marcello

Palazzo
Bembo
e Boldù

Palazzo
Priuli

Palazzo
Cavagnis

5

Osteria alle
Testiere

Palazzo
Donà

Santa Maria
della Fava

Campo
Santa Maria
Formosa

Palazzo
Grimani

Ex Ospizio
Sa
Loren

Palazzo
Faccanon

Santa Maria
Formosa

Fondazione
Querini
Stampalia

Campo
San Lorenzo

San
Zulian

Palazzo
Tasca-Papafava

Palazzo
Soranzo

Palazzo
Zorzi

S Giovanni
in Oleo

Palazzo
Priuli

Palazzo Zorzi
Da Remigio

Torre dell'
Orologio

Palazzo
Trevisan

Palazzo
Patriarcale

Museo dei Dipinti
Sacri Bizantini

San Giorg
degli Grec

Procuratie
Vecchie

Piazza
San Marco

Basilica di
San Marco

Museo Diocesano
d'Arte Sacra

San
Zaccaria

6

Caffè
Quadri

Campanile

PONTE
DEI SOSPIRI

Palazzo
Dandolo

Museo
Civico Correr

Palazzo
Ducale

Palazzo
Prigioni

Convento

Caffè
Florian

Museo
Archeologico

Palazzo
Reale

Palazzo
Ducale

PONTE
DELLA
PAGLIA

Riva degli
Schiavoni

Santa Maria
della Visitazione
o della Pietà

Palazz
Navager

Procuratie
Nuove

Giardini
ex Reali

Libreria
Sansoviniana

Piazzetta
San Marco

Leone di
San Marco

PONTE
DEL VIN

San Zaccaria
(Piazza San Marco)

San Marco
(MVE)

Capitaneria
di Porto

Zecca

S Teodoro

Ridotto

San Marco

San Marco
(Vallaresso)

7

0   300 m

0   300 yds

H   J   K

96

San Francesco
della Vigna

x Chiesa
S Giustina

Palazzo
Gritti o della
Nunziatura

Campo
Giustina

Palazzo
lazzo Contarini
adenigo

C S Francesco

Campo della
Confraternita

F Case Nuove

C d Oratorio

C d Cimitero

C te del
Muneghe

Celestia

Rio d S Francesco

Campo
o Celestia

C te
d Morion

Campo
S Ternita

Rio d Celesta

C d Vida

C Nuova

x Convento

San Giovanni
dei Cavalieri
di Malta

C dell'Olio

Campo
S Ternita

Canale delle Galeazze

Scuola di
San Giorgio
degli Schiavoni

Rio d S Ternita

Palazzo
Magno

Campo
S Gatte

C tlo
tue Pozzi

Osteria
Oliva Nera

S Antonino

Corte
Soranze

C te
d Angelo

Darsena Arsenale Vecchio

Darsena
Grande

Piszina S Martin

Corte
Venier

C te Gorne

C d Gorne

San
Martino

Arsenale

n Giovanni
in Bragora

Corte
Sconta

Fond dl Fronte

Torri
dell'Arsenale

C Erizzo

Campo
Arsenale

CASTELLO

degli Schiavoni

Ca' di Dio

Campo
della
Tana

Arsenale

Riva Ca' di Dio

Ex Forni

Museo
Storico
Navale

Palazzetto
dello Sport

Rio della Tana

Fond della Tana

Fond della Tana

S Francesco
di Paolo

Campo
S Biagio

Riva S Biagio

San Biagio

Via Giuseppe Garibaldi

Monumento
a Garibaldi

Canale   di   San   Marco

Riva del Sette Martiri

Giardini
Garibaldi

L

M

N

Castello Quick Reference Guide

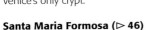

San Zaccaria (▷ 44)

San Zaccaria dates from the ninth century, though what you see now, essentially two adjacent churches, is a blend of both Gothic and Renaissance styles. Inside, look out for Giovanni Bellini's *Madonna and Child with Saints* (1505), and don't miss the chance to inspect Venice's only crypt.

Santa Maria Formosa (▷ 46)

This interesting church and its *campo* is archetypical Venice—diverse architecture, a lively square that's the hub of the neighbourhood, and one of Venice's most beguiling museums. The Byzantine 11th-century church was altered in 1492 by Mauro Codussi in the new Renaissance style.

Santi Giovanni e Paolo (▷ 54)

This huge Gothic preaching church is typical of those built by the mendicant religious orders, with a cavernous interior designed to accommodate huge crowds. It's the burial place of more than 20 doges, and contains some of the city's best sculpture. The highlights are on the west wall.

Scuola di San Giorgio degli Schiavoni (▷ 60)

Tucked away on a side canal, this charitable *scuola* is home to some of the most charming paintings in the city, a cycle by Carpaccio, painted in the first decade of the 16th century. You'll recognize St. George slaying the dragon, while the terrified princess looks on.

CITY TOURS

Sunrise over the Riva degli Schiavoni

San Polo and Santa Croce

Enclosed by a loop of the upper stretches of the Canal Grande, the west-bank *sestieri* of San Polo and Santa Croce are densely populated, workaday districts, where there's a tangible sense of Venice as a living city. The Rialto, with its superb fish and fruit and vegetable markets, is the focus, with the big sights mainly lying south of here, among them fine churches and museums, while the whole area has good shopping and great bars and restaurants.

Morning
Start your day—and miss the worst of the crowds—by taking the *vaporetto* along the **Canal Grande** (▷ 20–21; right), alighting at San Tomà, the nearest stop to the great church of **Santa Maria Gloriosa dei Frari** (▷ 48–49), where you'll find plenty to fill in 40 minutes or so.

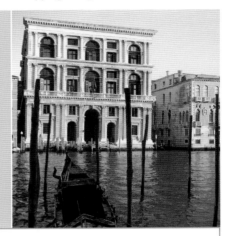

Mid-morning
You'll find good choices for a mid-morning stop on the Campo dei Frari—try **Bottega del Caffè Dersut** (▷ 146), where there are delicious smoothies, as well as excellent coffee, on offer. Then stroll round the side of the Frari to take in the mind-blowing architecture, incredible interior decoration and superb paintings by Tintoretto in the **Scuola Grande di San Rocco** (▷ 58–59).

Lunch
You could follow the main route up towards the Rialto and sit beside the Canal Grande for lunch at **Bancogiro** (▷ 146; left), where there's a choice of *cichetti* (Venetian-style tapas) as well as a full menu. Alternatively, choose somewhere in Campo San Polo, Venice's second largest square.

Afternoon

After lunch, you'll want to browse the stalls around the **Rialto bridge** (▷ 38–39), good trawling ground for gifts and souvenirs. Later, take the *vaporetto* towards Piazzale Roma from Rialto Mercato, and get off at San Stae, from where you can visit two important museums, **Ca' Pesaro** (▷ 66–67), a magnificent *palazzo* housing the city's modern art collection, or **Palazzo Mocenigo** (▷ 70–71; left), home to a fascinating collection of costumes displayed in a great palace.

Mid-afternoon

From Palazzo Mocenigo it's a short stroll to **San Giacomo dell'Orio** (▷ 71–72; right), a fascinating church on a *campo* that's a good place to sit and relax with a drink. Explore the little streets around here, where you'll find tiny specialist shops and hidden corners.

Evening

If you haven't already taken it in, you can cut through from here to Campo San Polo to take in the church of **San Polo** (▷ 73–74) before joining the locals who congregate here for the early evening *passeggiata*.

Dinner

There's a great choice of restaurants to suit all tastes and pockets in the area—go upmarket and enjoy stunning modern cuisine at the **Antiche Carampane** (▷ 146), head for **Alla Madonna** (▷ 144), one of Venice's most famous and traditional fish restaurants, or enjoy an excellent pizza at **Il Refolo** (▷ 150), back on Campo San Giacomo dell'Orio.

2

0 ————————— 300 m
0 ————————— 300 yds

Parco di
Savorgnan

Tempio
Israelitico

Palazzo
Nani

C. d. Forno

Canale di Cannaregio

Fond S Giobbe

C d Case Nuove

C d Riello Vecchio

Rio Terra S Leonardo

C d Cendon

C te delle due oss

C te
Cendon

Palazzo
Savorgnan

C de Pesaro

Palazzo
Venier

Guglie

PONTE
D GUGLIE

Campo
S Leonardo

Ex Chiesa
di San Leonardo

C d Mosto Balbi

C Carmelitani

C Priuli ai Cavalletti

C d Misericordia

C te Canal

Palazzo
Zeno

C te Pesaro

Rio Terra S Leonardo

3

STAZIONE
VENEZIA
SANTA LUCIA

Chiesa degli
Scalzi

Ferrovia

Fond S Lucia

Ferrovia

Ponte
degli Scalzi

Fond di Scalzi

Rio Terra Lista di Spagna

Palazzo
Calbo-Crotta

Fond Crotta

Palazzo
Foscari

Palazzo
Flangini

San Geremia
e Lucia

Campo
S Geremia

Palazzo
Labia

Palazzo
Emo

Riva de
Biasio

Riva di Biasio

Palazzo
Corner

Palazzo
Gritti

Palazzo
Donà-
Balbi

Canal Grande

San Geremia

Palazzo
Marcello
Toderini

Palazzo
Giovane

Palazzo
Correr
Contarini

Palazzo
Gidoni-
Bembo

San Giovan
Decollad

C Larga

Case
Contarini

S Simeon
Piccolo

Palazzo
Adoldo

C llo di
Comare

Campo
S Simeon
Grando

Campo
S Simeon
Profeta

S Simeon
Grando

Campo
N Sauro

Il Réfolo

San Giacomo
dell'Orio

Campo S
Giacomo
dell'Orio

Ruga Bella

C d Savio

Fond S Simeon Piccolo

Fond S Simeon Grando

C d Traghetto

Ramo Chioverete

Palazzo
Gradenigo

Palazzo
Soranzo
Cappello

C te Cristo

Palazzo
Mariani

4

Ponte della
Costituzione
(Calatrava)

Palazzo
Emo-Diedo

Palazzo
Papadopoli

Giardino
Papadopoli

C te casa Nuove

Campo d Lana

C d Tabacco

Campo N Sauro

Rio di S Zuane

Scuola Grande di
San Giovanni
Evangelista

C d Strope

Campo d
Anatomia

Rio di S Giacomo d Orio

Palazzo
Zane-Collalto

Palazzo
Giustinian

Palazzo
Molin

SANTA
CROCE

Palazzo
Condulmer

Piazzale
Roma

Campazzo
Tre Ponti

Fond Madazen

Lavadori

C d Clero

Campo d
Tolentini

San Nicolò
da Tolentino

San Giovanni
Evangelista

Campo
S Stin

Palazzo
Zen

Ro Terra S Tomà

5

Fond Rizzi

Fond dei Rio Novo

Fond Minotto

Palazzo
Marcello

Fond di Cattaro

Fond Tolentini

Salizz S Pantalon

Rio di Muneghette

C te
Spirti

Archivio
di Stato

San
Rocco

C llo d
Castelforte

Santa Maria
Gloriosa dei Frari

Campo
S Rocco

Campo
dei Frari

C te
Baddor

Fond Pagani

Palazzo
Gabrielli Dolfin

C d Galio

Scuola
Grande
di San
Rocco

Bottega del
Caffè Dersut

Museo Casa Carl
Goldor

Campo
S Tomà

S Tomà

Palazzo
Dolfin

Fond del Rio Novo

San
Pantaleone

Campo
S Pantalon

Palazzo
Signolo
Loredan

C d Brett

Palazzo Marcello
dei Leoni

Palazzo
Civran Grimani

Santa
Tomà

Palazzo
Contarini
delle Figure

6

Palazzo
Cicogna

Fond Bratti

Fond S Soccorso

Institutio Superiore
d'Arte Applicata

Santa Maria
dei Carmini

Collegio
Armeno

Scuola Grande
dei Carmini

Campo Santa
Margherita

Scuola
dei Varòtari

Rio Terra S Scoazzera

PONTE
DEI PUGNI

Rio di S Barnaba

Campo
San Barnaba

San Barnaba

Ca' Rezzonico

Palazzo
Nani
Bernardo

Palazzo
Grassi

San
Samuele

Campo
S Samuele

Ca'
Rezzonico

Contarini-
Michiel

Palazzo
Stern

Palazzo
Moro

Palazzo
Loredan

Ca' del
Duca

Palazzo Falier

Palazzo
Foscarini

Fond Foscarini

Santa
Margherita

Palazzo
Giustinian

Ca' Foscari

Palazzo
Balbi

Palazzo
Da Lezze

Palazzo
Morolin

D

E

Sacca della Misericordia

C.llo dei Servi di Maria

Cappella del Volto Santo

Palazzo Diedo

S Marziale

S Marziale

La Maddalena

S Fosca

Palazzo Vendramin-Calergi (Casinò)

Palazzo Correr Contarini

Palazzo Giovanelli

Fondaco dei Turchi

Canal Grande

Palazzo Belloni Battagia

Museo di Storia Naturale

Ca' Tron

San Stae

Palazzo Priuli-Bon

San Stae

Museo del Tessuto e del Costume

Palazzo Agnus Dio

Ca' Pesaro

Palazzo Donà

Palazzo Corner della Regina

Casa Favretto

Ca' d'Oro

Palazzo Mocenigo

Santa Maria Mater Domini

Palazzo Zane

San Cassiano

Palazzo Grioni

Palazzo Moro

Palazzo Gozzi

Palazzo Muti-Baglioni

Antiche Carampane

Fabbriche Nuove

Fabbriche Vecchie

Gobbo

San Giovanni di Rialto Elemosinario

Bancogiro Rialto

S Giacomo di Rialto

Erberia dei Tedeschi

Rialto

Palazzo Bernardo

Palazzo Albrizzi

Palazzo Molin-Cappella

Sant' Aponal

SAN POLO

Palazzo Soranzo

Palazzo Maffetti-Tiepolo

San Polo

San Silvestro

Canal Grande

Ponte di Rialto

San Bartolomeo

Palazzo Dolfin-Manin

Scuola Grande di San Teodoro

Palazzo Corner Mocenigo

Campo San Polo

Palazzo Barzizza

Palazzo Ravà

San Silvestro

Teatro Goldoni

San Salvador

Palazzo Donà della Madonnetta

Palazzo Papadopoli

Palazzo Donà

Palazzo Corner Martinengo

Teatro

Mercerie

Palazzo Corner

Palazzo Pisani-Moretta

Palazzo Grimani

Palazzo Bernardo

Palazzo Cappello-Layard

Palazzo Benzon

San Benedetto

San Luca

Palazzo Barbarigo

Palazzo Tiepolo

Palazzo Persico

Sant'Angelo

Palazzo Corner-Spinelli

Teatro Rossini

Palazzo Contarini dei Cavalli

Palazzo Grimani

San Benedetto

Palazzo Curti

Santa Toma

Palazzo Mocenigo

Museo Fortuny

Oratio dell'Annunziata

Palazzo Contarini del Bovolo

Ateneo Veneto

SAN MARCO

San Gallo

Museo Civico Correr

Puntalaguna

Santo Stefano

Campo Santo Stefano

San Maurizio

Santa Maria del Giglio

Teatro La Fenice

San Moisè

San Vidal

Palazzo Morosini

Palazzo Zaguri

Scuola Vecchia della Misericordia

S Maria Valverde

Scuola Nuova della Misericordia

Palazzo Lezze

Palazzo Molin

Palazzo Papafava

Ex Chiesa di Santa Caterina

Palazzo Vendramin

S Felice

Palazzo Boldù

Palazzo Fontana

S Sofia

Ca' d'Oro

Palazzo Foscari Sagredo

S Sofia

Palazzo Michiel delle Colonne

Santi Apostoli

Scuola dell'Angelo Custode

Pescheria

Ca' da Mosto

Palazzo Lion-Morosini

Fondaco dei Tedeschi

Dieci Savi

Alla Madonna

Palazzo Dandolo

Palazzo Bembo

Palazzo Farsetti

Palazzo Loredan

CITY TOURS

103

San Polo and Santa Croce
Quick Reference Guide

Canal Grande (▷ 20)

If you do nothing else in Venice, take a *vaporetto* trip down this iconic waterway, which winds for 4km (2.5 miles) from Piazzale Roma to the glories of San Marco, with a spectacular pageant of some of the world's most beautiful buildings rising from the water on either side. Spanned by four bridges, the canal is lined with *palazzi* and churches whose architecture spans many styles.

Santa Maria Gloriosa dei Frari (▷ 48)

This impressive church, dating from the 13th century, was built for the Franciscans. Completed around 1395, the lofty interior contains masterpieces by some of Venice's greatest artists. Don't miss Titian's *Assumption of the Virgin* over the high altar, his *Madonna di Ca' Pesaro* in the left aisle, or Giovanni Bellini's triptych of the *Madonna and Child* in the sacristy.

Scuola Grande di San Rocco (▷ 58)

This headquarters of a charitable institution, or *scuola,* built 1515–49, was designed by Bartolomeo Bon. The interior is the perfect backdrop for the mind-blowing pictures by Tintoretto. His 54 paintings, on two floors, are one of the world's most impressive picture cycles by a single artist. Other works are by Titian, Giorgione, Bellini and Tiepolo.

CITY TOURS

Dorsoduro

Lying to the southwest of the Canal Grande, Dorsoduro's name means 'hard back', referring to the firm land on which it stands. Its southern boundary is the Giudecca canal, edged by the long stretch of the sunny Zattere, its hub, lovely Campo Santa Margherita. It's a compelling *sestiere*, with three important galleries, superb churches, *palazzi* and *campi*, while the University lends a buzz and ensures good shopping, lively bars and a choice of restaurants.

Morning
You could start your day early with an overview of Venetian painting by taking in the **Gallerie dell'Accademia** (▷ 24–25). Be sure to climb the steps of the **Ponte dell'Accademia** (▷ 71; right) for one of the finest of all Venetian views, down the Canal Grande towards Santa Maria della Salute.

Mid-morning
Wend your way eastwards through picturesque *calli* and *campi* to the **Collezione Peggy Guggenheim** (▷ 22–23) where you could have a drink at the excellent café before taking in the *palazzo* and the art collections. From here, it's a short walk to the **Punta della Dogana** (▷ 36–37; left) and the church of **Santa Maria della Salute** (▷ 52–53).

Lunch
From Santa Maria della Salute it's a pleasant stroll along the Zattere, where there are plenty of lunch choices. Turn off at Rio San Trovaso for the **Cantina del Vino Già Schiavi** with its fine range of *cichetti* (a Venetian version of tapas), or head east to **Osteria 1518** (▷ 149), where you can sit outside and sample traditional Venetian cooking.

Afternoon

Head back to **Ca' Rezzonico** (▷ 18–19) for a taste of hedonistic 18th-century interior design, before an afternoon trawling the charming backstreets of Dorsoduro. You could head to **San Sebastiano** (▷ 42–43; left), with its great Veronese paintings, or take in the lower-key charms of the contrasting churches of **San Nicolò dei Mendicoli** (▷ 73) or the **Angelo Raffaele** (▷ 66).

Mid-afternoon

Aim to finish your stroll by heading past the **Squero di San Trovaso** (▷ 74) to the Zattere, where you can buy one of the city's best ice creams at **Nico** (▷ 149), to enjoy on a bench looking across to the Giudecca.

Evening

Hit the tempting shops, to buy or browse, before heading to **Campo Santa Margherita** (▷ 67; left) where you can sit with a drink outside **Orange** (▷ 137), or one of the other bars, and soak up the atmosphere of this most appealing *campo*.

Dinner

Dorsoduro has restaurants for every taste and pocket, but among the nicest is **Montin**, a long-established and famous restaurant with a beautiful garden, that specializes in traditional Venetian cuisine elegantly served. Then it's time for a nightcap—the **Zattere** is lovely at night with the lights of the Giudecca twinkling across the water.

Santa Chiara

Piazzale Roma

Palazzo Emo-Diedo

Ponte della Costituzione (Calatrava)

Palazzo Soranzo Cappello

Campo S Andrea

Autorimessa

STAZIONE AUTOBUS

Palazzo Papadopoli

Giardino Papadopoli

Scuola Grande San Giova Evangelis

Ex Chiesa di Sant'Andrea

Piazzale Roma

San Giovan Evangelis

SANTA CROCE

Palazzo Condulmer

San Nicolò da Tolentino

Santa Mar Glorio dei Fra

San Rocco

Palazzo Marcello

Ex Fabbrica Tabacchi

Campo Tre Ponti

Palazzo Gabrielli Dolfin

Scuola Grande di San Rocco

Ex Chiesa di Santa Maria Maggiore

San Pantaleone

Palazzo Signole Loredan

S Teresa

Palazzo Foscarini

Santa Margherita

Campo Santa Margherita

Scuola dei Varotari

Orange

Scuola Grande dei Carmini

Ca' Rezzonico

Institutio Superiore d'Arte Applicata

San Barnaba

Palazzo Cicogna

Santa Maria dei Carmini

Campo San Barnaba

San Nicolò dei Mendicoli

Collegio Armeno

Angelo Raffaele

Campo Angelo Raffaele

San Sebastiano

DORSODURO

Ospedale G B Giustinian

Palazzo Brandolin

STAZIONE MARITTIMA

Ognissanti

Montin

Osteria 1518

San Trovaso

Palazzo Molin

San Basilio

STAZIONE MARITTIMA

Squero di San Trovaso

Fond Zattere al Ponte Lungo

S Mar d Visitazion

Zattere

Nico

Canale della Giudecca

Fond d Dolfini

Campo S Biagio

Campo d Lavraneri

Mulino Stucky

Isola della Giudecca

S Eufemia

Palanca Giudecc

Ex Convento delle Convertite (Penitenziario Femminile)

Campo S Cosmo

Ex Chiesa Santi Cosma e Damiano

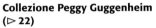

SIGHTS AND EXPERIENCES

Ca' Rezzonico (▷ 18)
Come to this magnificently opulent *palazzo* for a glimpse of the lifestyle of the 18th-century Venetian nobility.

Collezione Peggy Guggenheim (▷ 22)
Get an overview of all the main artistic movements of the second half of the 20th century.

Gallerie dell'Accademia (▷ 24)
An intimate gallery that takes you through the development of Venetian painting and showcases the work of the greatest painters.

Punta della Dogana (▷ 36)
This stunningly restored building, the best of 21st-century design, is home to changing exhibitions of cutting-edge contemporary art.

San Sebastiano (▷ 42)
A church that's a shrine to the great painter Veronese, who decorated virtually the entire interior.

Santa Maria della Salute (▷ 52)
This landmark church was built in the 18th century following an outbreak of the plague in Venice.

Scuola Grande dei Carmini (▷ 56)
See some of Tiepolo's best work in this intimate setting, designed by Baldassare Longhena.

Further Afield

Venice's lagoon, 50km (31 miles) long, is scattered with numerous other islands, and most visitors spend time exploring at least some of them. These two itineraries explore the best, and both will need forward planning as *vaporetti* run less frequently to outlying areas.

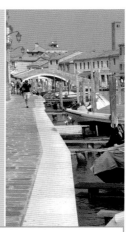

DAY 1
Morning
Start your day with a visit to **Murano** (▷ 28–29; right), taking the DM from Piazzale Roma or Ferrovia, or a boat from the Fondamente Nove. If you take this route, you could hop off for a short visit to the fascinating cemetery island of **San Michele** (▷ 69). On Murano, be sure to visit one of the glass factories, where you can watch glass-blowers at work, or visit the **Museo del Vetro** (▷ 29) to learn more. Then take the LN *vaporetto* from the Faro stop for the 40-minute journey to **Burano** (▷ 76).

Lunch
Burano has a good choice for lunch; try **Da Romano** (tel 041 735 217) or **Al Gatto Nero** (tel 041 730 120) both renowned for fish. After lunch, take a stroll round Burano, perhaps stopping off at the **Museo del Merletto** (▷ 76).

Afternoon
Back at the *vaporetto* stop, catch the T service for the short hop to **Torcello** (▷ 62–63), where you can visit the **Basilica di Santa Maria Assunta** (▷ 63; left) and church of **Santa Fosca** (▷ 63). You'll have to take the T line back to Burano to return to Venice.

Evening
The nicest route back to the city is the LN via Treporti and Punta Sabbioni, which gives you a chance to see more of the lagoon en route to the Lido. Change *vaporetti* here to return to Venice, either before or after dinner.

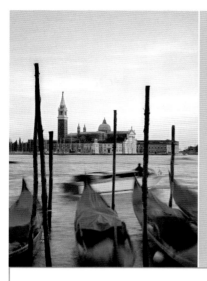

DAY 2
Morning
Catch *vaporetto* No. 2 to **San Giorgio** (▷ 40–41; left) to visit Palladio's superb church, starting by taking the lift up the campanile for views over Venice and the lagoon islands. From June to mid-September, the No. 2 runs from San Giorgio to the **Lido** (▷ 76), where you're heading next. During other months, you'll have to return to San Zaccaria and change onto the No. 1.

Lunch
Once on the Lido, there's plenty of choices for lunch on and just off the Gran Viale, which runs across the island from the lagoon to the open Adriatic. The Lido's **beaches** are a big draw; some have private facilities and are ticket only, others free, so you could have a swim and a couple of hours on the beach

Afternoon
Alternatively, take the 51 to the Fondamente Nove, where you connect with the No. 13 to the island of **Sant'Erasmo** (▷ 76; right). Here, you can walk for miles through vegetable fields and beside the lagoon. Disembark either at Capannone—if you want a good long walk, or Chiesa, and simply follow your nose along the island to eventually catch the boat back to Venice from the Punta Vela stop.

Fávaro V

Tessera

Mestre

CASONA

BISSUOLA

la Cerva

Aeroporto
Marco Polo

VIA ORLANDA

VIA BISSUOLA

Canale Osellino

VIA PIAVE

VILLAGGIO
S MARCO

VIA MARTIRI DELLA LIBERTÀ

Calzavara

Pu
Lun

Stazione
Venezia Mestre

Campalto

Padua,
Vicenza

VIA D. LIBERTÀ

Porto di
Compalto

Marghera

Isola di
Tessera

VIA FLLI BANDIERA

Choggia

S Giuliano

Isola di
Campalto

Laguna

PONTE DELLA LIBERTÀ

Sacca
Serenella

I S Secondo

Isola di
San Michele

Porto
Marghera

Stazione
Venezia
Santa Lucia

Cimitero

I del Tronchetto

I d Tresse

VENEZIA

Moranzani

Canale della Giudecca

Navíglio Brenta

Canale Bondante
di Sotto

Isola
San Giorg
Maggio

Fusina

I S Giórgio
in Alga

Isola della
Giudecca

I La Grázia

Veneta

I S Ángelo

I S Clemente

Sacca
Séssola

I S Spirito

CA'BIANC

Lago
dei
Téneri

Laguna

Isola Forte
di Sopra

Isola
Povéglia

Isola Forte
di Mezzo

MALAMOCCO

Isola Forte
di Sotto

L di Rívola

0   4 km

ALBERONI

0   2 miles

Porto di
Malamocco

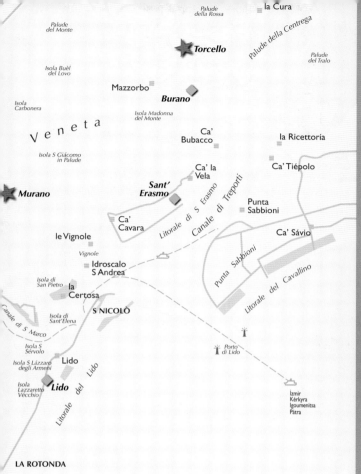

la Cura

Palude
della Rossa

Palude della Centrega

Torcello

Palude
del Tralo

Palude
del Monte

Isola Buèl
del Lovo

Mazzorbo

Burano

Isola
Carbonera

Isola Madonna
del Monte

Ca'
Bubacco

la Ricettoría

V e n e t a

Isola S Giácomo
in Palude

Ca' la
Vela

Ca' Tiépolo

Murano

Sant'
Erasmo

Litorale di S Erasmo

Punta
Sabbioni

Ca'
Cavara

Canale di Treporti

Ca' Sávio

le Vignole

Punta Sabbioni

Vignole

Idroscalo
S Andrea

Litorale del Cavallino

Isola di
San Pietro

la
Certosa

Punta Sabbioni

S NICOLÒ

Isola di
Sant'Elena

Canale di S Marco

Isola S
Sérvolo

Porto
di Lido

Lido

Isola S Lázzaro
degli Armeni

Isola
Lazzaretto
Vécchio

Lido

Litorale del Lido

İzmir
Kérkyra
Igoumenitsa
Pátra

LA ROTONDA

CITY TOURS

Murano (▷ 28)

Ten minutes by *vaporetto* from Venice, the island of Murano, complete with its own canals, churches and *palazzi*, has been the centre of Venetian glass manufacture since the Middle Ages. The Museo del Vetro tells the story and you can watch glass-blowing in the workshops. The beautiful 12th-century church of Santa Maria e Donato is another highlight.

San Giorgio Maggiore (▷ 40)

Across the Bacino di San Marco from the Palazzo Ducale, the little island of San Giorgio Maggiore (opposite) is dominated by the great Palladian church of the same name and its adjoining monastic buildings. Built between 1565 and 1610, the classical design shines with white marble and stucco, while the view from the campanile is one of Venice's finest.

Torcello (▷ 62)

More than an hour's journey from the city, in the wastes of the northern lagoon, once heavily populated Torcello is home to an exquisite ninth-century Basilica, the oldest complete building in Venice, famous for its superb Byzantine mosaics. The island is also home to the church of 11th-century Santa Fosca and a small museum.

MORE TO SEE	64

Burano
The Lido
Sant'Erasmo

Shop

Whether you're looking for the best local products, a department store or a quirky boutique, you'll find them all in Venice. In this section shops are listed alphabetically.

SHOP

Introduction

Venice was one of the world's greatest trading hubs for 500 years before its decline in the 17th and 18th centuries. Sumptuous goods from all corners of the globe filled its markets, shops and warehouses. Today, its trade is less exotic but often still tempting.

On Offer
Venice is a provincial city and its shops reflect this, though you'll find many designer names and some great Italian fashion, accessories and shoes. Transportation costs and high rents also mean prices are often higher than elsewhere.

Traditional Gifts
Venice's extraordinary history has bequeathed the city several unique shopping possibilities. The artisan traditions of Murano and Burano, for example, make glass and lace from these two lagoon islands good buys—though you need to be on your guard against inferior, foreign-produced products. Glass trinkets can also provide some of Venice's most kitsch souvenirs.

Beautiful Masks
With the revival of the Venice carnival in 1979, the last few years has seen shops selling and producing the traditional masks (*maschere*) worn by celebrants proliferating. Some masks are mass-produced—but often still beautiful—while others are painstakingly created by hand

BURANO LACE
Although lace was made by women of all classes during the Middle Ages, it was the development of an intricate stitch known as Burano point that made the eponymous island (▷ 76) famous for its lace. Mass production in the 19th century devastated the industry, and today only a handful of women make lace by hand. Much of what you see for sale in Burano and the rest of Venice is foreign- or machine-made. For the real thing you will have to search long and hard and be prepared to pay.

Clockwise from top: Masks hanging outside a shop; lace parasols in Burano; the Rialto fish market; a shop window display of Murano glass; hand-printed paper in

in workshops, such as Tragicomica (▷ 129) around the city. Locally produced masks fetch high prices, but they do make the most wonderful souvenirs.

Stationery Delights
Marbled paper, another traditional Venetian craft, has also enjoyed a revival since the 1970s and shops across the city sell a range of paper products. The craft is almost 1,000 years old, and spread from Japan to Persia and the Arab world during the Middle Ages. It reached Europe in about the 15th century. Mass-produced papers are perfectly good, but the best buys are authentic, made using old hand- and woodblock-printing techniques.

Delicate Materials
Shops selling a host of fine silks, damasks and other fabrics reflect the city's trading days. And as you'd expect in a city with such an illustrious artistic past, there are many antiques shops filled with beautiful paintings, prints and objets d'art (▷ panel, 125).

And to Eat
Food souvenirs include pasta in every shape and form, rice and polenta, olive oil, dried *porcini* (mushrooms), vinegars, spices and traditional Burano biscuits.

SHOP

MURANO GLASS

Glass-making began in Venice in Roman times, but took off in the 13th century, when foundries were moved to Murano (▷ 28–29) to lessen the risk of fire. Today, the island is a key production area; though shops sell Murano glass everywhere in Venice, the best choice, and keenest prices, are on the island. With its ornate forms and many tints, Murano glass is an acquired taste but the huge variety of styles includes both contemporary and traditional designs. At its best, glass is one of the city's most distinctive buys.

---

a range of designs; the view from the Rialto bridge towards Campo San Bartolomeo

Directory

San Marco

Books and Stationery
Ebrû
Goldoni
Legatoria Piazzesi
Paolo Olbi
Il Papiro
Fabrics
Colorcasa
Fashion
Ciocca
Fiorella
Prada
Jewellery and Beads
F. G. B.
Nomination
Shoes and Accessories
Pelleteria Maria
Pied à Terre
Souvenirs
Galleria Livio de Marchi

Cannaregio

Books and Stationery
Gianni Basso
Food and Drink
Ballarin
Fashion
Camicissima

Castello

Books and Stationery
Libreria Acqua Alta
Jewellery and Beads
Anticlea Antiquariato
Muranero
Fabrics
Marco Polo
Fashion
Barbieri Arabesque
Glass
Pauly
Shoes and Accessories
La Padovana

San Polo and Santa Croce

Books and Stationery
Legatoria Polliero
Food and Drink
Aliani Gastronomia
Casa del Parmigiano
Drogheria Mascari
Fashion
Balocoloc
Hibiscus
Zazù
Souvenirs
Emilio Ceccato
Gilberto Penzo
Tragicomica

Dorsoduro

Art and Antiques
Bac Art Studio
Books and Stationery
Libreria Toletta e Toletta Studio
Food and Drink
Pantagruelica
Glass
Marina & Susanna Sent
Souvenirs
Mondo Nova

Shopping A-Z

ALIANI GASTRONOMIA

Perhaps Venice's most famous delicatessen, this shop has a superlative selection of cheeses, together with a variety of hams, salamis, fresh pasta and other ready-made delicacies—all perfect for a picnic.

🔲 G5 ⊠ Ruga Vecchia San Giovanni, San Polo 654 ☎ 041 522 4913 ➲ Rialto or San Silvestro N, 1, 2

ANTICLEA ANTIQUARIATO

This beautiful little shop is a wonderful collection of antique Venetian beads and jewellery. The owner has spent a lifetime amassing her stock, the best of which is kept in countless small drawers around the walls. Beads of your choice can be made up, while you wait, into earrings or necklaces.

🔲 K6 ⊠ Campo San Provolo, Castello 4719a ☎ 041 528 6946 ➲ San Zaccaria 1, 2, 41, 42, 51, 52

BAC ART STUDIO

www.bacart.com

For some stunning photos of Venice to take home and prove to people that it really does look dreamlike, Bac Art Studio has an impressive range. There are also framed prints of original art, as well as stationery and calendars.

🔲 F7 ⊠ San Vio, Dorsoduro 862 ☎ 041 522 8171 ➲ Accademia N, 1, 2

BALLARIN

This excellent *pasticceria* has a superb range of cakes and pastries, to sample with a cup of coffee or take out. It also makes delicious chocolates and sweets—look out for the chocolate-coated orange peel, candied fruit and fresh cream chocolate truffles.

🔲 H4 ⊠ Salizzada San Giovanni Crisostomo, Cannaregio 5794 ☎ 041 528 5273 ➲ Rialto N, 1, 2

BALOCOLOC

www.balocoloc.com

All the hats sold here are original and handmade by the owner, Silvana Martin, who changes her designs to suit the season. There are lovely brimmed hats, doge-like knitted ones in bright designs and some pretty berets. You can take

Confectionery in a shop window on Campo San Luca

SHOP

123

your time and have a real rummage while Silvana sits making up her creations in the background. The shop also stocks costumes for the Carnevale at better prices than some of the more well-known shops. There is a second outlet in Cannaregio at Strado Nova 326.

➕ G4 ✉ Calle Longa, Santa Croce 2134
☎ 041 524 0551 or 041 640 273 🚤 San Silvestro N, 1, 2

BARBIERI ARABESQUE

This elegant shop sells nothing but scarves, stoles and pashminas in silk, wool, cashmere and a great range of hues and styles; all tracked down by the English-speaking owner, who has excellent contacts in the silk-weaving towns around Lake Garda. Scarves for dressing up, keeping you warm and adding individuality and luxury to any outfit.

➕ K6 ✉ Ponte dei Greci, Castello 3403
☎ 041 522 8177 🚤 San Zaccaria 1, 2, 41, 42, 5, 52

CAMICISSIMA

There are permanent bargain prices here on men's shirts, beautifully tailored in pure cotton and poplin—Italian style in a huge range of fabric designs and colours. Buy four for under €110.

➕ G3 ✉ Rio Terra della Maddalena, Cannaregio 1367 ☎ 041 275 0925
🚤 San Marcuola 1, 2

CASA DEL PARMIGIANO

www.aliani-casadelparmigiano.it
A stone's-throw from the Rialto markets, this little family-run shop sells superb cheese, *salumeria* (delicatessen) from all over Italy and light-as-a-feather home-made fresh pasta. Locals consider this one of the best shops in Venice, so be prepared to stand in line.

➕ H5 ✉ Erberia, San Polo 214–15
☎ 041 520 6525 🚤 Rialto N, 1, 2

CIOCCA

www.ciocca.it
Northern Italy is renowned for its knitwear, and Ciocca has a superb range, with sweaters, cardigans, jackets and accessories in yarns that range from ultra-fine merino through cashmere to chunky thick wool, ideal for outerwear.

➕ H6 ✉ Calle dei Fabbri, San Marco 1066
☎ 041 522 7156 🚤 Rialto 1, 2

COLORCASA

This shop is crammed with some of the most sumptuous decorating fabrics you can imagine—silks, brocades and figured velvets are for sale by the length or made up into cushions, drapes and bags. Silk key tassels and curtain swags are equally tempting, and ColorCasa stocks wonderfully warm *trapunti* (quilted bed-covers) in vivid fabrics.

➕ F5 ✉ Campo San Polo, San Polo 1989–91 ☎ 041 523 6071 🚤 San Tomà N, 1, 2

SHOP

MARIANO FORTUNY

Fortuny was born in Catalonia, Spain in 1871, the son of a painter and fabric collector. He moved to Venice when he was 18, soon gaining renown in fields ranging from physics and chemistry to architecture and theatre design. Today, he is best remembered for his fabrics, and in particular for the pleated dresses he created that were so fine they could be rolled up and threaded through a wedding ring.

DROGHERIA MASCARI

www.imascari.com

On the 'street of spice merchants' near the Pescheria (fish market), this wonderful shop, crammed with interesting foods, spices, dried fruit and nuts, teas, coffees and sweets, also has nicely wrapped packets of dried mushrooms, jars of truffles, balsamic vinegar and beautiful biscuits. It's a great place for that take-home foodie souvenir.

🔲 G4 ✉ Ruga dei Spezieri, San Polo 382 ☎ 041 522 9762 🚊 Rialto or San Silvestro N, 1, 2

EBRÛ

The owner of this shop, Alberto Valese, was at the cutting edge of the 1970s revival in Venetian marbled paper. His shop takes its name from the traditional Turkish marbling technique used to create many of his products. Some small items make ideal gifts or souvenirs.

🔲 F6 ✉ Campo Santo Stefano, San Marco 3471 ☎ 041 523 8830 🚊 Giglio 1

EMILIO CECCATO

If there is one souvenir, over and above glass, that greets you at every turn in Venice, it is the fake and mass-produced gondolier's straw hat. This unique little shop sells the genuine article, together with gondoliers' garb—hats, tunics and trousers—to both gondoliers and curious foreigners.

🔲 H5 ✉ Sottoportego di Rialto, San Polo 1617 ☎ 041 522 2700 🚊 Rialto N, 1, 2, 4

F.G.B.

This long-established store, housed in a charming *casinetto* in the centre of the *campo*, sells all the traditional Venetian souvenirs at some of the best prices in town.

ANTIQUES

Bric-a-brac and antiques bargains are rare in a city that is acutely aware of its past and the value of its objets d'art. Still, Venice provides an almost unlimited choice of beautiful things to buy. The most famous shops in San Marco are Paolo Scarpa's two outlets at Campo San Moisè, San Marco 1464 (🔲 H6) and Calle Larga (Viale) XXII Marzo, San Marco 2089 (🔲 H6).

There are glass pieces in clear and milk colours, beads and earrings, paper products and much more besides, and there's plenty for children that won't break the bank.

🔲 G7 ✉ Campo Santa Maria del Giglio, San Marco 2514 ☎ 041 523 6556 🚊 Giglio 1

FIORELLA

www.fiorellagallery.com

Hilarious and original, Fiorella has Venice's best-dressed window: The wooden shop dummies represent life-size models of former doges, each decked out in high heels and other offbeat high fashion items.

🔲 F6 ✉ Campo Santo Stefano (Campo Francesco Morosini), San Marco 2806 ☎ 041 520 9228 🚊 Accademia N, 1, 2

GALLERIA LIVIO DE MARCHI

www.liviodemarchi.com

You will probably see examples of Livio de Marchi's work as you walk around Venice: everyday objects such as socks, umbrellas or hanging shirts lovingly and precisely carved of wood. You may not want to buy the items, but the works are unique, and great fun.

🔲 F6 ✉ Salizzada San Samuele, San Marco 3157/a ☎ 041 528 5694 🚊 Sant'Angelo or San Samuele N, 1, 2, 4

Beautiful Venetian handmade paper

prints, posters and simple models (perfect for children) either as kits or ready-made and painted.

➕ F5 ✉ Calle II Saoneri, San Polo 2681 ☎ 041 719 372 🚣 San Tomà N, 1, 2

GOLDONI

Well stocked and by common consent the best general bookshop in Venice, Goldini has a wide range of literature on the city, along with a limited selection of English and other foreign-language titles.

➕ H6 ✉ Calle dei Fabbri, San Marco 4742 ☎ 041 522 2384 🚣 Vallaresso N, 1, 2

GIANNI BASSO

Going into Gianni Basso's *stampatore* will take you back in time. The huge old printing presses are still in action, making business cards for people all over the world. Gianni has resisted change—he doesn't have a fax or website and takes orders by mail only. He also sells beautiful lithographs of Venice then and now.

➕ J2 ✉ Calle del Fumo, Cannaregio 5306 ☎ 041 523 4681 🚣 Fondamente Nove 1, N, 13, 25, 41, 42, 51, 52

GILBERTO PENZO

What more appropriate gift or souvenir to take home from Venice than a gondola? This shop sells beautiful handmade wooden models of the boats, as well as gondola

HIBISCUS

A rainbow of hot Indian hues shines in the great selection of ethnically inspired scarves, jackets, bags and jewellery in this tempting store, a wonderful, if expensive, contrast to the vast number of cheap glass and mask shops in this area. The clothes are well cut and comfortable, and the stock changes continually.

➕ G5 ✉ Ruga Rialto, San Polo 1060–61 ☎ 041 520 8989 🚣 San Silvestro 1

LEGATORIA PIAZZESI

Established in 1900, this is one of the last workshops in the city to use traditional wood-block methods to hand-print its exceptionally fine papers, books and stationery.

➕ G6 ✉ Campiello della Feltrina, San Marco 2511 ☎ 041 522 1202 🚣 Giglio 1

DEPARTMENT STORE

The only large department store worthy of the name is the excellent Coin, which sells a wide range of fashion, toiletries, accessories, china, linen, gifts and general goods. The staff win the prize for being among the most engaging shop assistants in Venice. It occupies a large corner block on the east side of Salizzada San Giovanni Crisostomo 5790 between the Rialto and the church of San Giovanni Crisostomo (➕ H4). Visit Coin Beauty at Campo Santa Luca for endless beauty bargains.

SHOP

This small but atmospheric market (🕐 Mon–Sat 8–1), just outside the north gates of the Via Garibaldi (gardens), sells fish, *salumeria* (cooked and cured meats), fruit and vegetables. If you are visiting the Museo Storico Navale or the Biennale, it is worth taking a look and enjoying a relatively tourist-free experience; if you're buying, prices are among the city's lowest.

LEGATORIA POLLIERO
This tiny, old-fashioned shop alongside Santa Maria Gloriosa dei Frari, offers a lovely selection of leather-bound and marbled paper stationery, together with hand-made gifts and beautiful individual sheets of paper.
➕ F5 ✉ Campo dei Frari, San Polo 2995 ☎ 041 528 5130 🚤 San Tomà N, 1, 2

LIBRERIA ACQUA ALTA
This shop is a one-off, with its cluttered interior dominated by a gondola serving as a book display stand, and its walls stacked high with new and second-hand books. The multilingual owner is an enthusiast; unsurprisingly, the accent of the stock is on Venice, and you'll also find photos, posters and a selection of gifts.
➕ J5 ✉ Calle Longa Santa Maria Formosa, Castello 5176 ☎ 041 296 0841 🚤 San Zaccaria 1, 2

LIBRERIA TOLETTA E TOLETTA STUDIO
The Libreria is an excellent bookshop with a huge range of coffee-table books on Venice, guidebooks, Italian classics, art and cookery books—and they're all offered with good discount. Across the *calle*, the Studio has more art books, posters, T-shirts and small gifts suitable for souvenirs.
➕ E7 ✉ Calle Toletta, Dorsoduro 1214 ☎ 041 523 2034 🚤 Ca' Rezzonico

MARCO POLO
Bruno Tagliapietra is renowned for his sumptuous and beautiful hand-blocked and figured damask velvets, made in the traditional Venetian style. Deeply and richly coloured fabric is made up into cushions, runners, bedspreads, stoles and scarves—a souvenir to hand on to the next generation.
➕ M7 ✉ Via Garibaldi, Castello 1696 (if closed ask at Castello 1764 for access) ☎ 041 523 2716 🚤 Arsenale 1, 41, 42

MARINA & SUSANNA SENT
www.marinaesusannasent.com
For a more contemporary take on Murano glass, this shop has funky vases, plates and jewellery that won't break the bank. They sell lovely glass pebbles, too.
➕ F7 ✉ Campo San Vio, Dorsoduro 669 ☎ 041 520 8136 🚤 Accademia N, 1, 2

MONDO NOVO
www.mondonovomaschere.it
The masks in this shop, just south of Campo Santa Margherita, are definitely superior to the mediocre versions in lesser shops around the city. This is a wonderful place for children and adults alike.
➕ E6 ✉ Rio Terrà Canal, Dorsoduro 3063 ☎ 041 528 7344 🚤 Ca' Rezzonico 1

MURANERO
Niang Moulaye from Senegal became fascinated with Venetian

SHOP

glass-making when he came to Italy as a student. He learned the craft of bead-making and today makes beautiful, solid necklaces and bracelets in intense colours, the earthy or vibrant shades and designs inspired by Africa.

➕ L6 ✉ Salizada del Pignater, Castello 3545 ☎ 347 649 7947, 338 450 3099 🚤 Arsenale 1, 41, 42

NOMINATION
www.nomination.it

Nomination is a nationwide Italian firm that makes distinctive, modern, well-designed jewellery at affordable prices. Hinged bracelets in silver and chrome set with semi-precious stones are the hallmark pieces, but the range has expanded and there are plenty of temptations.

➕ H5 ✉ Calle Goldoni, San Marco 4609 ☎ 041 520 1344 🚤 Rialto 1, 2

LA PADOVANA
This leather store pulls in locals and visitors, all attracted by the classic, middle-range shoes, boots and accessories for men and women. They are not at fashion's cutting-edge but well made and you'll find seasonal numbers.

THE RIALTO

As a district, the Rialto is almost as old as the city itself, the earliest settlers having been attracted to its high banks, or *rivo alto*, which formed a dry and easily defended redoubt amid the marsh and mud of the lagoon. While San Marco developed into the city's political heart, the Rivoaltus became its commercial hub, where all manner of staple and exotic goods were traded in the 'Bazaar of Europe'.

➕ J6 ✉ SS Filippo e Giacomo, Castello 4272 ☎ 041 522 4106 🚤 San Zaccaria 1, 2

PANTAGRUELICA
Pantagruelica is arguably the finest food shop in Venice, offering the best produce from all over Italy. The emphasis is on quality, with plenty of organic produce featured on the shelves. The enthusiastic owner is always happy to spend time talking about the food producers he patronizes.

➕ E6 ✉ Campo San Barnaba, Dorsoduro 2844 ☎ 041 523 6766 🚤 Ca' Rezzonico 1

PAOLO OLBI
Another artisan at the forefront of the revival of marbled paper, Olbi's appealing shop sells marbled stationery and ornaments that make the perfect gift.

➕ G6 ✉ Calle della Mandola, San Marco 3653 ☎ 041 528 5025 🚤 Sant'Angelo 1, 2

IL PAPIRO
A fine little shop, with branches around the world, selling marbled paper as well as handsome desk objects, cards, notebooks, diaries and other pretty stationery. There are two other outlets in the city.

➕ G6 ✉ Calle del Piovan, San Marco 2764 ☎ 041 522 3055 (all shops) 🚤 Giglio 1

PAULY
Pauly has been selling the finest Venetian glass since 1866. Its warren of showrooms contain all manner of treasures. There is also an outlet on the Piazza San Marco.

➕ G3 ✉ Ponte Consorz Calle Largo, Castello 4391 ☎ 041 520 9899 🚤 All services to San Zaccaria

PELLETERIA MARIA

There's a huge range of bags, wallets and purses here, all leather, all made in Italy and all at excellent prices. Designs and colours change as fashions come and go, but they always stock a good selection of classic bags both large and small.
➕ G6 ✉ Calle Spezier, San Marco 2630
☎ 041 523 7814 🚤 1 Giglio

PIED À TERRE

www.piedaterre-venice.com
This tiny shop, behind the market stalls at the foot of the Rialto bridge, has the best selection in Venice of *furlani*, lovely velvet slippers that come in myriad jewel-bright colours, with non-slip soles made of recycled bicycle tyres—comfortable, hard-wearing and quintessentially Venetian.
➕ H4 ✉ Ruga d'Orefici, 60 Rialto/San Polo 60 ☎ 041 528 5513 🚤 Rialto Mercato 1

PRADA

You'll find no less than three Prada outlets opposite the church of San Moisè, two carry clothes, bags and accessories from the mainstream collections of this iconic designer, while the other houses a branch of Miu Miu, Prada's younger, sharper sister store.
➕ H6 ✉ Salizada San Moisè, San Marco 1469 ☎ 041 528 3966 🚤 San Marco Vallaresso, San Marco Giardinetti, Giglio

TRAGICOMICA

www.tragicomica.it
Superb handmade masks, created by an artist trained at Venice's Accademia delle Belle Arti, echo the 18th-century heyday of *Carnevale*. Look for Harlequins, Columbines and pantaloons, the plague doctor and some imaginative mythological masks.
➕ F5 ✉ Calle dei Nomboli, San Polo 2800 ☎ 041 721 102 🚤 San Tomà N, 1, 2

ZAZÙ

Women can wear the clothes from Zazù anywhere, anytime; fabrics are natural and the cut is beautiful, with items such as voluminous trousers tapering at the ankle, draped tops, and bias-cut skirts in softest jersey, all style trademarks. Strong colours are used as accents alongside grey and black, or tones of sand and off-white.
➕ F5 ✉ Calle dei Saoneri, San Polo 2750 ☎ 041 715 46 🚤 San Tomà 1, 2

SHOP

PRACTICALITIES

Food shops and bakeries are usually open 8.30–1 and 4–7, though virtually all close on Wednesday afternoon and Sunday. For locals, mornings are set aside for food shopping and this is the time to visit the city's markets at the Rialto and the locality, which open around 8.30. Food served by weight (including bread) is sold by the *chilo, mezzo chilo* (kilo and half-kilo; about 2lb and 1lb) and, more commonly, by the *etto* (100g; about 4oz), plural *etti*.

Entertainment

Once you've done with sightseeing for the day, you'll find lots of other great things to do with your time in this chapter, even if all you want to do is relax with a drink. In this section establishments are listed alphabetically.

Introduction

If Venice is beautiful beyond words by day, at night it's possibly still lovelier. With the day trippers gone, most streets and alleys away from the main squares are eerily quiet, perfect for a late stroll in the velvet summer darkness.

Night-time Enchantment

Most visitors to Venice have only a few nights to enjoy the city's night-time atmosphere, and there's no better way to do so than take a walk off the beaten track. Venice is one of the safest cities in the world, so you should have no worries about exploring its dark streets. Wherever you go, you'll find yourself ambling through an atmospheric world of medieval corners and narrow streets that open up to views enhanced by the combination of darkness and artificial light. Moonlight glistens on the water and the only sounds are distant, echoing footsteps and the slap of water on stone—magical indeed. Round it off with a nightcap or copy the natives and buy a *gelato* (ice cream) to enjoy as you go.

What's On

All very well for a few nights, but the evening may come when you're looking for entertainment. It has to be said the choice is limited, and you won't find clubs, pubs and thumping music: Venice goes to bed

---

DARK WATERS

Few things are more enchanting than a trip down the Canal Grande under a starlit sky. Indeed, it is almost worth organizing your arrival in the city for nightfall, so that you can approach your hotel by *vaporetto* or water taxi under the cover of darkness: It may be the most memorable part of your trip. And if you are going to lavish a small fortune on a gondola ride, make sure it is at night. Better still, take it in the silent, dark-dappled canals away from the main waterways.

Clockwise from top: Live music entertains patrons of Caffè Florian; the Canal Grande; a couple standing near fairy lights on a canal bridge; viewing artists' work on

remarkably early. Scattered throughout the city, though, are late-night bars, many with live music at least two or three times a week, and a handful of clubs. Follow the students to Campo Santa Margherita, where there's plenty of late action, or head to northern Cannaregio, where the Fondamenta della Misericordia has a string of late-opening bars. For something a bit more elegant, you could hit the tables at the Casino, housed right on the Canal Grande in a stunning *palazzo*.

The Cultural Scene

Many visitors take advantage of Venice's cultural life, surprisingly vibrant for what is, in essence, a small provincial city. There are concerts of Venetian music virtually every evening somewhere in the city, many featuring performers dressed in 18th-century costumes to play Vivaldi against the backdrop of some beautiful *salone* in a sumptuous *palazzo*. The opera season at the wonderful Fenice runs from September until June, and city theatres often stage concerts and occasional dance performances.

To see what's on while you're there, pick up a copy of the free day-by-day listings magazine, *Eventi e Manifestazione*, published every three months and available from tourist information offices.

VALUE FOR MONEY

If you're watching the purse, you can have a great-value evening by taking a *vaporetto* trip up or down the Canal Grande and alighting at San Marco or the Accademia. From San Marco you can stroll along the Riva degli Schiavoni, with its fabulous evening views, while the Accademia stop gives access to the Zattere, a sheltered quayside with views to the Giudecca, benches and Nico's (▷ 149), one of the best *gelaterie*. Other options include taking a picnic to the Lido, window-shopping in the upmarket streets of San Marco, or great people-watching.

Piazza San Marco; Basilica di San Marco illuminated in the dark; a night-time view from Ponte dell'Accademia

Directory

San Marco

Live Entertainment
Venezia the Show
Music Clubs and Bars
Bacaro Jazz
Haig's Bar
Torino@Notte
Vino Vino
Theatre, Opera and Classical Music
Musica in Palazzo
Teatro La Fenice

Cannaregio

Live Entertainment
Casinò Municipale di Venezia
Music Clubs and Bars
Algiubagio
Paradiso Perduto
Zenevia
Theatre, Opera and Classical Music
Teatro Fondamente Nuove
Teatro Malibran
Cinema
Cinema Multisala Giorgione Movie D'Essai

Castello

Music Clubs and Bars
Giorgione

Theatre, Opera and Classical Music
Fondazione Querini Stampalia

San Polo and Santa Croce

Cinema
Arena di Campo San Polo
Music Clubs and Bars
Bagolo
Caffè dei Frari
Do Mori
Theatre, Opera and Classical Music
Chiesa di San Giacometto
Palazzetto Bru Zane
Santa Maria Gloriosa dei Frari
Scuola Grande di San Giovanni Evangelista

Dorsoduro

Music Clubs and Bars
Cantina del Vino già Schiavi
Orange
Piccolo Mondo
Round Midnight
Suzie Café
Theatre, Opera and Classical Music
Santa Maria della Salute

Entertainment A-Z

ALGIUBAGIO
www.algiubagio.net
Right by the *vaporetto* landing stage, this busy, modern and welcoming bar is a good place for a warming or reviving drink and snack while waiting for, or after disembarking from a boat. Or drop by during a stroll around the farther reaches of Cannaregio.

⊞ J3 ⊠ Fondamente Nuove, Cannaregio 5039 ☎ 041 523 6084 ⊙ Wed–Mon 7am–midnight ⛴ Fondamente Nove 41, 42, 51, 52

ARENA DI CAMPO SAN POLO
For six weeks from late July to early September this large *campo* is transformed into an open-air cinema, attracting audiences of up

to 1,000 people. The backdrop of flickering hues across crumbling Venetian buildings adds to the drama. Films, mainstream and festival hits, are usually dubbed into Italian.

🚹 F5 ✉ Campo San Polo, San Polo ☎ 041 524 1320 🕓 Phone for latest details 🚢 San Silvestro 1, San Tomà N, 1, 2

BACARO JAZZ
www.bacarojazz.com
The fabulous Cuban *barista* (barman) here does his utmost to make you feel welcome, and more importantly mixes a mean *mojito*. Expect plenty of jazz and *gondolieri* enjoying themselves. There is good food, too.

🚹 H5 ✉ Salizzada del Fontego dei Tedeschi, San Marco 5546 ☎ 041 528 5249 🕓 Thu–Tue 4pm–3am 🚢 Rialto N, 1, 2

BAGOLO
Located on a pretty and tucked-away square with small cafés, bars and restaurants, Bagolo is an atmospheric place to drink, particularly with its low lighting and candlelit tables out on the *campo* in summer.

🚹 F4 ✉ Campo San Giacomo dell'Olio, Santa Croce 1584 ☎ 041 717 584 🕓 Tue–Sun 8–2 🚢 Riva de Biasio 1, 51, 52

CAFFÈ DEI FRARI
This is a great place for an aperitif, especially if you want to dine nearby. Many Venetians start their night with the house spritz or a glass of Prosecco.

🚹 F5 ✉ Fondamenta dei Frari, San Polo 2564 ☎ 041 524 1877 🕓 Daily 8am–9pm. Closed 15 days in Aug 🚢 San Tomà N, 1, 2

CANTINA DEL VINO GIÀ SCHIAVI
Here is an old-fashioned wine bar that really looks the part, set almost opposite San Trovaso and one of Venice's few remaining gondola workshops.

🚹 E7 ✉ Fondamenta Nani-Meravegie, Dorsoduro 992 ☎ 041 523 0034 🕓 Closed Sun pm 🚢 Accademia or Zattere N, 1, 2, 51, 52, 61, 62

CASINÒ MUNICIPALE DI VENEZIA
www.casinovenezia.it
Venice's popular Casinò Municipale (Municipal Casino), one of only a handful in Italy, is housed in the impressive Palazzo Vendramin-Calergi. Dress code is smart—a jacket and tie for men. Guests must be over age 18 and bring ID.

🚹 F3 ✉ Palazzo Vendramin-Calergi, Calle Larga Vendramin, off Rio Terrà della Maddalena, Cannaregio 2040 ☎ 041 529 7111 🕓 Daily 2.45pm–2.30am 🚢 San Marcuola N, 1, 2 💷 Expensive

CHIESA DI SAN GIACOMETTO
www.prgroup.it
This intimate church of San Giacomo di Rialto, affectionately

---

EVENING PASTIMES

Venice does not have the nightlife to match other major cities. For many Venetians an evening out consists of a meal or drink with friends rounded off with a stroll to a bar for a coffee or ice cream. One of the best places to join them is in squares such as Campo San Polo (🚹 F5). *Scuole* and churches are also popular for classical music concerts.

known as San Giacometto, near the Rialto markets is considered by many to be the oldest in Venice. It hosts frequent concerts by the Ensemble Antonio Vivaldi and other guest orchestras.

➕ H4 ✉ Campo di San Giacometto, San Polo 30125 ☎ 041 426 6559 ⏰ Phone or visit website 🚢 Rialto, San Silvestro 1

CINEMA MULTISALA GIORGIONE MOVIE D'ESSAI

A good selection of art-house films is shown at this two-screen Cannaregio cinema. Hollywood films are often dubbed into Italian.

➕ H4 ✉ Rio Terrà dei Franceschi, Cannaregio 4612 ☎ 041 522 6298 ⏰ Phone for latest details 🚢 Ca' d'Oro N, 1

DO MORI

The most authentic and atmospheric of Venice's old-time *bacari* (▷ panel; below) has been in business since 1462. It's always bustling with people from the nearby Rialto markets. It serves good snacks and stock 350 wines. All guests must stand.

➕ G4 ✉ Calle do Mori, off Ruga Vecchia San Giovanni, San Polo 429 ☎ 041 522 5401 ⏰ Mon–Sat 8.30–8.30 🚢 Rialto N, 1, 2

FONDAZIONE QUERINI STAMPALIA

www.querinistampalia.it

This cultural institution organizes a diverse selection of artistic events, with regular Friday and Saturday classical concerts held in the opulent surroundings of a 15th-century *palazzo salone*.

➕ J5 ✉ Campiello Querini Stampalia, Castello 5252 ☎ 041 271 1411 ⏰ Hours vary 🚢 Rialto N, 1, 2 and all services to San Zaccaria

GIORGIONE

Venetians flock to this trattoria-cum-pizzeria for the quality food, Friulian wines and Venetian folk music. The owner, Lucio Bisutto, is one of the art's leading exponents and frequently performs his all-singing and a little dancing 'fisherman's tales from the *osterie*'.

➕ M7 ✉ Via Giuseppe Garibaldi, Castello 1533 ☎ 041 522 8727 ⏰ Closed Wed 🚢 Giardini N, 1, 41, 42, 51, 52, 61, 62

HAIG'S BAR

Haig's is an American-style piano bar and part of the Giglio restaurant, popular with visiting Americans and young locals—and those locals who wish they were younger! You'll enjoy very good, but slightly pricey, Venetian fare.

➕ G7 ✉ Campo Santa Maria del Giglio, San Marco 5277 ☎ 041 528 9456 ⏰ Daily 11.30–3, 7–2 🚢 Giglio 1

MUSICA IN PALAZZO

www.musicapalazzo.com

Watch grand opera on a chamber music scale in the evocative

WINE BARS

Old-fashioned wine bars, or *bacari,* are a Venetian way of life. One of the city's more civilized habits is the custom of breaking up the day with an *ombra* ('shadow'), a small glass of wine that takes its name from the idea of escaping the heat of the sun for a restorative tipple. A small snack, or *cichetto*, usually accompanies the drink. An *enoteca* is a more refined bar, with a greater choice of wines and a range of reasonably priced snacks and hot meals.

surroundings of an 18th-century *palazzo*. Performances of some best-loved operas, such as *La Traviata* and *The Barber of Seville*, take place in the state rooms of the palace, with performers singing their roles among the audience.

⊞ G7 ✉ Palazzo Barbarigo Minotto, Fondamenta Barbarigo, San Marco 2504 ☎ 39 340 971 7272 🕐 Peformances daily 8.30pm 🚤 Giglio 1

ORANGE

www.orangebar.it

Orange spritz is the signature drink here in this orange-themed bar, restaurant and champagne lounge. There's an upstairs terrace, to watch life on the Campo, but most of the achingly chic drinkers are too busy watching each other.

⊞ E6 ✉ Campo Santa Margherita, Dorsoduro 3054/a ☎ 041 523 4740 🕐 Daily 8am–2am 🚤 Ca' Rezzonico 1

PALAZZETTO BRU ZANE

www.bru-zane.com

The Palazzetto Bru Zane opened in 2008 as the venue for around 100 concerts annually, all themed to aspects of the 19th-century French Romantic movement, either a composer, a specific instrument or a musical theme. This is a good contrast to Venice's staple musical diet of 18th-century Italian offerings. Some concerts are given in the Scuola Grande di San Rocco.

⊞ E4 ✉ Calle dell'Ogio, San Polo 2368 ☎ 041 521 1005 🕐 Telephone or check website for times and schedules 🚤 San Tomà, Piazzale Roma

PARADISO PERDUTO

The atmosphere at this renowned nightspot makes up for the fairly

average food that is served here. The inexpensive wine and eclectic music attract a diverse, alternative crowd, and its legendary all-night theme parties have ruffled many locals' feathers over the years.

⊞ G2 ✉ Fondamenta della Misericordia, Cannaregio 2640 ☎ 041 720 581 🕐 Tue–Sun 11–3, 6–2 🚤 Madonna dell'Orto 41, 42, 51, 52

PICCOLO MONDO

This may not be the most hip, and it is probably the smallest, but Piccolo Mondo is one of Venice's few music clubs.

⊞ F7 ✉ Calle Contarini Corfù, Dorsoduro 1056/a ☎ 041 520 0371 🕐 Tue–Sun 11pm–4am 🚤 Accademia N, 1, 2

ROUND MIDNIGHT

This intimate club attracts all sorts for the mainstream music.

⊞ E6 ✉ Calle dei Pugli, off Fondamenta dello Squero, Dorsoduro 3102 ☎ 041 523 2056 🕐 Mon, Wed–Sat 10pm–4am 🚤 Ca' Rezzonico 1

SANTA MARIA GLORIOSA DEI FRARI

www.chorusvenezia.org
www.basilicadeifrari.it

There are sacred music concert

Bright lights in Riva degli Schiavoni

series in spring and autumn, sometimes featuring orchestral ensembles, other times organ recitals. The church makes a great setting for music.

🚇 E5 ⊠ Campo dei Frari, San Polo 🕾 041 522 2637 🕐 Phone for latest details 🚢 San Tomà N, 1, 2

SANTA MARIA DELLA SALUTE

This is the venue for a variety of classical organ music. As well as performances by the lead organist of the basilica, guest performers also appear as part of Sunday Mass at 11am every week.

🚇 G7 ⊠ Campo della Salute, Dorsoduro 1 🕾 041 522 5558 🕐 Phone for latest details 🚢 Salute 1

SCUOLA GRANDE DI SAN GIOVANNI EVANGELISTA

www.scuolasangiovanni.it

The stunning main hall of this important Scuola Grande the backdrop for spring and autumn performances of some of Italy's best-loved operas. Book online or buy your tickets at the door.

🚇 E5 ⊠ Campiello della Scuola, San Polo 2454 🕾 041 426 6559 🕐 Feb–May, Sep–Oct; telephone or check website for times and schedules 🚢 San Tomà, Piazzale Roma

SUZIE CAFÉ

Popular with students in the day, this place transforms into a swinging bar at night. On Friday nights live jazz groups, or reggae and funk bands perform.

🚇 D7 ⊠ Campo San Basegio, Dorsoduro 1527A–B 🕾 041 522 7502 🕐 Mon–Thu 7–7, Fri–Sat 8am–1am (if there's a concert in the *campo*) 🚢 Zattere N, 1, 2, 51, 52, 61, 62

TEATRO LA FENICE

www.teatrolafenice.it

This famous opera house (▷ 75) hosts a full schedule of operas and other concerts, and you can also join a daytime tour to see the fabulous interior.

🚇 G6 ⊠ Campo San Fantin, San Marco 1965 🕾 041 786 500; information 041 2424 or 041 786 511; for tickets www.hellovenezia.it 🚢 Giglio 1

TEATRO FONDAMENTE NUOVE

www.teatrofondamentenuove.it

Venice's premier avant-garde venue, wonderfully set on the

WHAT'S ON

Details of films, concerts and exhibitions in Venice are listed in the 'Spettacoli' section of daily editions of local newspapers such as *Il Gazzettino* and *La Nuova Venezia*. *Un Ospite di Venezia*, a free Italian/English magazine available from hotels and tourist offices, also contains detailed listings (published weekly in peak season, monthly during the off season). Tourist offices always have plenty of posters and leaflets on current events (▷ 133). Also keep an eye open for posters on the streets.

northern lagoon in remote Cannaregio, was founded in 1993 in an old joiners' shop. Teatro Fondamente Nuove stages contemporary dance and organizes performances, film festivals, workshops and exhibitions as part of its innovative Art and Technology project, which explores the relationship between artistic creativity and technology.

➕ J3 ✉ Fondamente Nuove, Cannaregio 5013 ☎ 041 522 4498 ⏰ Phone for latest details 🚤 Fondamente Nove 1, N, 13, 25, 41, 42, 51, 52

TEATRO MALIBRAN

www.teatrolafenice.it

A theatre has stood on this site since 1677, and the Teatro Malibran was Venice's most elite performance venue throughout the 18th century. Today it stages well-known operas such as *La Traviata* and more modern works, as well as classical concerts and first-class ballet productions.

➕ H4 ✉ Calle dei Milion, Cannaregio 5873 ☎ 041 786 603; box office 041 786 601 ⏰ Phone for latest details 🚤 Rialto N, 1, 2

TORINO@NOTTE

Live jazz, beer, spritz and toasted sandwiches make up the staple diet of the fun-loving crowd here. The action spills out onto the *campo* during the summer and during carnival.

➕ H5 ✉ Campo San Luca, San Marco 459 ☎ 041 522 3914 ⏰ Tue–Sat 7.30pm–1am 🚤 Rialto N, 1, 2

VENEZIA THE SHOW

www.teatrosangallo.net

If you want an entertaining look at the history of Venice, the nightly shows here combine live action with state-of-the-art video, music and sound presentations to evoke the history of the city and the atmosphere of Carnival—touristy, but good fun.

➕ H6 ✉ Campo San Gallo, San Marco 1097 ☎ 041 241 2002 ⏰ Performances daily 7pm 🚤 San Marco Vallaresso, San Marco Giardinetti 1, 2 💶 Expensive

VINO VINO

Rather more showy and smarter than some of Venice's humbler bars, this two-roomed spot close to the opera house has more than 100 different wines to accompany its snacks and meals.

➕ G6 ✉ Ponte delle Veste, Calle delle Veste, San Marco 2007a ☎ 041 241 7688 ⏰ Wed–Mon 10.30am–midnight 🚤 Giglio 1

ZENEVIA

This bar is popular for its intimate nooks inside and its seating outside on Campo Santa Maria Formosa. Giant spritz and Guinness are consumed by an up-for-it crowd. There is occasional live music.

➕ J5 ✉ Campo Santa Maria Formosa, Cannaregio 5548 ☎ 041 520 6266 ⏰ Wed–Mon 9pm–2am 🚤 Zattere, Rialto

---

WHERE TO GO

Nightlife in Venice is decidedly low key. Late-night possiblilities are really limited to bars and live-music cafés, where you can hear jazz, blues or reggae, with the occasional Latino or rock session. A main party area is Fondementa della Misericordia in Cannaregio, where a string of waterfront bars and tiny clubs transforms the whole quayside into one long nightspot.

Eat

There are places to eat across the city to suit all tastes and budgets. In this section establishments are listed alphabetically.

Introduction

Food in Venice is glorious, but it can also be dire, so steer away from places offering a *menù turistico* and be prepared to pay more than you might expect. Venetian cooking is based on fish, game and vegetables, with the accent on fish and seafood.

When to Eat
Breakfast is usually served between 8 and 10. Locals often pop into a bar on their way to work for a cappuccino and a *briosc* (pastry). Venetian restaurants popular with locals operate two timescales—one for them and one for visitors. Working Venetians eat lunch between 12 and 1 and dinner between 8 and 9. Restaurants aimed mainly at tourists start lunch at 12.30 and dinner at 7, though some serve throughout the day.

Where to Eat
Like many Italian cities, there is a confusing array of eating places. A *ristorante* tends to be expensive, whereas the trattoria is less formal, less expensive, and often family-run. Such places may not have a printed menu, and the waiter will reel off a list of what's on offer; many speak enough English to help you choose. *Osterie* were basic, and some still are, but the term is often synonymous with good food and rustic elegance. *Pizzerie* in Venice tend to open all day; ovens are electric so Venetian *pizze* aren't as good as in Rome or Naples.

WHAT TO EAT

A full Venetian meal is gargantuan—*antipasti,* a *primo* (first course) of soup, rice or pasta, a *secondo* (main course) of fish with vegetable *contorni* (side dishes), then *formaggi* (cheese) and *dolce* (pudding). Do as the locals do and pick and mix. Few Venetians eat either cheese or pudding in restaurants, preferring to head for a *pasticceria* or choose a *gelato* (ice cream) if they want something sweet to round off a meal.

From the top: Caffè Florian; fritelle (small doughnuts) are a popular snack; outdoor tables at Caffè Florian; the stunning Murano glass chandelier at Caffè Quadri

EAT

Directory

San Marco

Cafés and Bars
Caffè Florian
Teamo
Fine Dining
Harry's Bar
Fish and Seafood
Acquapazza
Al Conte Pescaor
Ice Cream
Paolin
Trattorias and *Osterias*
Osteria al Bacareto
Osteria ai Rusteghe

Cannaregio

Trattorias and *Osterias*
Osteria l'Orto dei Mori
Venetian
Anice Stellato
Trattoria Cea
Vini Da Gigio

Castello

Fish and Seafood
Al Mascaron
Corte Sconta
Trattorias and *Osterias*
Alla Rivetta
Da Remigio
Osteria alle Testiere
Osteria Oliva Nera

San Polo and Santa Croce

Cafés and Bars
Bottega del Caffè Dersut
Ciak
Fine Dining
Poste Vecie
Fish and Seafood
Da Ignazio
Italian
Antica Birraria la Corte

Pizzerias
Alle Oche
Muro Venezia Frari
Il Refolo
Trattorias and *Osterias*
Osteria la Zucca
Trattoria San Tomà
Venetian
Alla Madonna
Antiche Carampane
Bancogiro
Ribó

Dorsoduro

Cafés and Bars
Improntacafe
Fine Dining
Antica Montin
Ice Cream
GROM
Nico
Venetian
La Bitta
Dona Onesta
Osteria 1518
Taverna San Trovaso

EAT

Eating A–Z

ACQUAPAZZA €€–€€€

www.venicemasaniello.com

Sit outside on one of San Marco's nicer *campi* here. The accent is mainly on fish: Starters include prawns and rocket with balsamic dressing and a seafood platter; follow with the catch of the day or a fish risotto. They serve good pizza.

➕ G6 ✉ Campo Sant'Angelo, San Marco 3808 ☎ 041 277 0688 ⏰ Tue–Sun lunch and dinner. Closed Mon and Jan 🚣 Sant'Angelo

AL CONTE PESCAOR €€

A wonderful tiny fish restaurant that caters to Venetians, despite its proximity to Piazza San Marco.

➕ J6–H6 ✉ Piscina San Zulian, San Marco 544 ☎ 041 522 1483 ⏰ Mon–Sat lunch and dinner. Closed Sun and Jan in winter 🚣 San Marco Vallaresso, San Marco Giardinetti N, 1, 2

AL MASCARON €€

www.osteriamascaron.it

This nice old bar-trattoria has a brisk, informal atmosphere, a beamed ceiling and black-and-white photos on the walls. Fish and seafood is served at the heavy wood tables on paper tablecloths. It is so popular (reservations are essential) that the owners have opened Alla Mascareta for wine and snacks at No. 5183.

➕ J5 ✉ Calle Lunga Santa Maria Formosa, Castello 5525 ☎ 041 522 5995 ⏰ Mon–Sat lunch and dinner. Closed Sun and mid-Dec to mid-Jan 🚣 Rialto N, 1, 2

ALLA MADONNA €€

www.ristoranteallamadonna.com

One the most authentic and one of the oldest restaurants in the city, this has the look of a Venetian restaurant of 30 years ago. It is a popular preference for business meetings and family celebrations. The food is rigorously Venetian.

➕ H5 ✉ Calle della Madonna, San Polo 594 ☎ 041 522 3824 ⏰ Thu–Tue lunch and dinner. Closed Wed and 2 weeks in Aug 🚣 Rialto N, 1, 2

ALLA RIVETTA €

An inexpensive but good, small trattoria close to Piazza San Marco that makes a pleasant alternative to some of the more expensive places. It is often very busy.

➕ J6 ✉ Ponte San Provolo, near Campo SS Filippo e Giacomo, Castello 4625 ☎ 041 528 7302 ⏰ Tue–Sun lunch and

---

WINES

Most of Venice's wine comes from the Veneto region on the mainland. Its best-known wines are the usually unexceptional Soave (white), and Valpolicella and Bardolino (reds). More interesting whites include Soave Classico, Bianco di Custoza, Tocai, Pinot Grigio and the wines of the Breganze region. The best white of all is Prosecco, a delicious dry sparkling wine often drunk as an aperitif. Interesting reds include Raboso, the wines of the Colle Berici and Lison-Pramaggiore regions, and two excellent dessert wines: Amarone and Recioto della Valpolicella.

EAT

Caffè Florian (▷ 147)

Fish, such as this turbot, and seafood are superb in Venice

dinner. Closed Mon and Aug All services to San Zaccaria

ALLE OCHE €–€€
Just south of quiet little Campo San Giacomo dell'Orio, this restaurant is very popular, so reserve or arrive early to secure a table outside, and enjoy a pizza.
 F4 Calle del Tintor, San Polo 1552 041 524 1161 Daily lunch and dinner Riva di Biasio 1

ANICE STELLATO €€
The lovely 'Star Anise' effortlessly combines its role as a down-to-earth neighbourhood *bacaro* (wine bar) with that of a rustically elegant trattoria serving traditional Venetian food. You may find the bar area packed with locals but, once at table, you can enjoy a delicious meal, its dishes entirely dependent on the season and what's in the market. For a light lunch, choose saucers of *cichetti* (snacks) from the array, with *ombra*, a glass of local white wine.
 F2 Fondamenta della Sensa, Cannaregio 3272 041 720 740

 Wed–Mon lunch and dinner. Closed Tue Sant'Alvise 41, 42, 51, 52

ANTICA BIRRARIA LA CORTE €€
This converted warehouse is one of a new breed of Venetian restaurants. The seating spills out into evocative Campo San Polo, making it perfect for sunny days and balmy evenings. The inside is contemporary, with clean lines and chrome. The food nods to all the Venetian and Italian classics—it's good quality. You can snack or go the whole hog here.
 F5 Campo San Polo, San Polo 2168 041 275 0570 Tue–Sun 11–3, 6–10 San Silvestro 1

ANTICA MONTIN €€
This venerable restaurant has been famous for decades and is popular with the rich and famous, although today it depends somewhat on its former reputation. The quality of food is now once again touching former heights; an evocative place to eat, either in the painting-lined dining room or on the shaded outside terrace to the rear.

EAT

E7 ✉ Fondamenta di Borgo, Dorsoduro 1147 ☎ 041 522 7151 🕔 Tue dinner, Thu–Mon lunch and dinner. Closed Wed 🚤 Zattere or Ca' Rezzonico N, 1, 2, 51, 52

ANTICHE CARAMPANE €€€

www.veneziaristoranti.it

One of the association of Buona Accoglienza restaurants, whose members aim to promote traditional Venetian cooking and hospitality, this off-the-beaten-track restaurant specializes in beautifully cooked, elegantly served seafood and fish. The style is a modern take on tradition, seen at its best in dishes such as *spaghetti alla granseola* (spaghetti with spider crab), *cassopipa* (pasta with a spicy fish sauce) or *branzino in salsa di peperoni* (sea bass in sweet pepper sauce). The wine list is long and interesting and desserts are light, elegant and imaginative. Booking is essential.
G4 ✉ Ponte delle Tette, San Polo 1911 ☎ 041 524 0165 🕔 Mon dinner, Tue–Sat lunch and dinner. Closed Sun 🚤 San Stae/Rialto Mercato

BANCOGIRO €€

www.osteriabancogiro.it

Housed in one of the 16th-century buildings around the markets, the Bancogiro is a well-run, laid back and welcoming restaurant that doubles as a bar serving *cichetti*. The menu relies on local, seasonal ingredients carefully prepared with a modern twist by chef Jacopo Scarso. The brick-vaulted interior is understated and elegant, and the outside tables are set right beside the Canal Grande.
H4 ✉ San Giacometto, San Polo 1220 ☎ 41 523 2061 🕔 Tue–Sun 12.30–3, 7–10. Closed Mon 🚤 Rialto Mercato 1

LA BITTA €€

La Bitta has an attractive bottle-filled dining room and internal courtyard, along its length. They serve mainly meat-based dishes.
E6 ✉ Calle Lunga San Barnaba, Dorsoduro 2753/a ☎ 041 523 0531 🕔 Mon–Sat dinner. Closed Sun 🚤 Ca' Rezzonico 1

BOTTEGA DEL CAFFÈ DERSUT €

Huge windows allow a glimpse into the interior of this popular café, where you can stand at the bar or relax on one of the deep sofas while you enjoy a speciality coffee—different flavours, different toppings, many laced with cream—or get a vitamin fix in the form of a blended veggie juice or mixed fruit smoothie made to order. They also serve pastries, tarts and cakes.
E5 ✉ Campo dei Frari, San Polo 3014 ☎ 041 303 2159 🕔 Daily breakfast, snacks all day 🚤 San Tomà

HARRY'S BAR

This famous bar and restaurant was founded in 1931 when, according to legend, a now-forgotten American ('Harry') remarked to hotel barman Giuseppe Cipriani that Venice lacked for nothing except a good bar. The enterprising Cipriani duly sought financial backing, found an old rope store near Piazza San Marco, and Harry's Bar was born. It is now a place of high prices, good food and great cocktails, and—in the words of writer Gore Vidal—'a babble of barbaric voices...the only place for Americans in acute distress to go for comfort and advice...'.

CAFFÈ FLORIAN €–€€€

The oldest, prettiest and most expensive of Venice's famous cafés has been serving customers since 1720. Prices are high, but treat yourself for the experience and the chance to admire the interior.

➕ H6 ✉ Piazza San Marco, San Marco 56–59 🕐 Thu–Tue breakfast, light lunch, snacks all day. Closed Wed 🚤 San Marco Vallaresso, San Marco Giardinetti N, 1, 2

CIAK €

A pleasant, relaxed bar, used by everyone from gondoliers to society ladies, to adjourn to after visiting Santa Maria Gloriosa dei Frari and the Scuola Grande di San Rocco. They do good lunchtime snacks and sandwiches.

➕ F5 ✉ Campo San Tomà, San Polo 2807 ☎ 041 528 5150 🕐 Daily breakfast, snacks all day 🚤 San Tomà N, 1, 2

CORTE SCONTA €€

www.veneziaristorante.it

Many Venetians and visitors alike rate Corte Sconta as their preferred restaurant, despite its slightly peripheral location. Fairly small and always busy, the cooking and seafood are rarely less than excellent. There is no menu, so try to follow waiting staff's recommendations. A garden has tables in summer.

➕ L6 ✉ Calle del Pestrin, Castello 3886 ☎ 041 522 7024 🕐 Tue–Sat lunch and dinner. Closed Sun–Mon 🚤 Arsenale 1, 41, 42

DA IGNAZIO €€

www.veneziaristorante.it

This fairly small, predominantly fish restaurant lies just east of Campo San Tomà, and has the atmosphere of a restaurant from the 1950s. There is a garden for alfresco dining in summer.

➕ F5 ✉ Calle Saoneri, San Polo 2749 ☎ 041 523 4852 🕐 Sun–Fri lunch and dinner. Closed Sat and 3 weeks in Jul and Aug 🚤 San Tomà N, 1, 2

DA REMIGIO €€

Small area trattorias are a dying breed in Venice, so this authentic restaurant, despite a redecoration that has removed some old-fashioned touches, is a find. It has just 40 seats, so you will need to reserve or arrive early to share a table. The food is reliable and homey, pasta and fish are good, and although the wine list is short it is adequate.

➕ K6 ✉ Salizzada dei Greci, Castello 3416 ☎ 041 523 0089 🕐 Wed–Sun lunch and dinner, Mon dinner. Closed Tue 🚤 Arsenale 1, 41, 42 or all services to San Zaccaria

DONA ONESTA €€€

www.donaonesta.com

The 'Honest Woman' lives up to its name with fine food at budget prices. It is becoming increasingly well known, however, so try to reserve a table in its single small dining room. Overlooks a little canal midway between San Pantalon and San Tomà.

THE COST

The bill (check; *il conto*) usually includes a cover charge per person *(pane e coperto)* and a 10–15 per cent service charge *(servizio)*. Restaurants are required by law to give you a proper receipt *(una ricevuta)*. Always look at your bill carefully, especially if—as still happens—it is an illegible scrawl on a piece of paper (strictly speaking illegal). Skipping *antipasti* and desserts will reduce costs—go to a *gelateria* for an ice cream instead.

EAT

A dessert of fried cream and sorbet

🔲 E5 ✉ Calle della Donna Onesta, Dorsoduro 3922 ☎ 041 710 586 🕐 Daily lunch and dinner 🚤 San Tomà N, 1, 2

GROM €
A nationwide chain, GROM has made a big impact with its ices. Flavours change monthly, and nothing is on offer unless it's in season. Coffee and salted caramel are particularly good. There is another branch at Strada Nuova (Ca' d'Oro), Cannaregio 3844.
🔲 E6 ✉ San Barnaba, Dorsoduro 2761 ☎ 041 099 1751 🕐 Daily 10–10 🚤 Ca' Rezzonico

HARRY'S BAR €€€
www.cipriani.com
This legendary establishment is best known for its celebrity status (▷ 146; panel). The restaurant upstairs serves reliable fare, while snacks can be ordered at the downstairs bar. This is *the* place for cocktails—the famous Bellini was invented here.
🔲 H7 ✉ Calle Vallaresso, San Marco 1323 ☎ 041 528 5777 🕐 Lunch and dinner. The bar is open every day but may close during carnival 🚤 San Marco Vallaresso, San Marco Giardinetti, N, 1, 2

IMPRONTACAFE €–€€
This part of town is university territory and this lively, well-designed modern bar and restaurant, with its late opening hours, pulls in crowds of students and young visitors. You can have breakfast, a light lunch, full dinner or just a drink, and find a buzzy atmosphere and fine choice of simple dishes. There's a good range of wines by the glass.
🔲 E5 ✉ Calle dei Preti Crosera, Dorsoduro 3815 ☎ 041 275 0386 🕐 Mon–Sat breakfast, lunch, dinner and snacks. Closed Sun 🚤 San Tomà 1, 2

MURO VENEZIA FRARI €–€€
Dark wood and minimalist design bring a feeling of space to this all-day bar-cum-eatery, where the menu offers a good range of *pizze* as well as standard Italian and Venetian dishes. It's convenient after a morning's sightseeing, reliable and relaxed.
🔲 F5 ✉ Rio Tera dei Frari, San Polo 2604b/c ☎ 041 524 5310 🕐 Fri–Wed lunch and dinner. Closed Thu 🚤 San Tomà

MORE OPTIONS

A fixed-price tourist menu *(menù turistico)* usually includes a basic pasta, main course, fruit and half-bottles of wine and water. Food quality is often indifferent—you will probably find many of the same dishes listed on the menu in a budget trattoria as in most expensive restaurants. The difference is primarily in ambience and detail. The *prezzo fisso* (fixed price) menu usually excludes cover, service and beverages. Check what is included in the price.

NICO €

Organize a walk in the Dorsoduro district so that you pass this small waterfront bar renowned for its ice cream, in particular a praline concoction known as *gianduiotto*.

🔒 E8 ✉ Zattere ai Gesuati, Dorsoduro 922 ☎ 041 522 5293 🕐 Fri–Wed breakfast, lunch and snacks. Closed Thu 🚢 Zattere N, 2, 51, 52, 61, 62

OSTERIA 1518 €€

Just off the west end of the Zattere, you'll find the 1518, whose tables spill outside in warm weather. Straightforward and unassuming, it prides itself on traditional Venetian cuisine served at honest prices. Expect fish from the market, a few meat dishes and watch for the set menus served at both lunch and dinner.

🔒 D7 ✉ Calle del Vento, Dorsoduro 1518/a ☎ 041 520 5799 🕐 Tue–Sun lunch and dinner. Closed Mon 🚢 San Basilio 2, 8, 51, 52

OSTERIA AL BACARETO €€

This well-placed traditional trattoria is in a quiet corner of the city just a few moments' walk west of the church of Santo Stefano. You can have a full meal, snack or a plate of antipasti with a glass of wine.

🔒 F6 ✉ Calle Crosera, San Marco 3447 ☎ 041 528 9336 🕐 Mon–Fri lunch and dinner, Sat lunch. Closed Sun 🚢 Sant'Angelo or San Samuele N, 1, 2

OSTERIA AI RUSTEGHI €

Venice is famous for its panini and *tramezzini* (filled rolls and sandwiches) and this tiny place offers well over 30 varieties, which you can enjoy with a beer or glass of wine from the long list. Sit in or outside on the *campo* and choose fillings ranging from scampi and rocket to full-flavoured porcini mushrooms and succulent beef.

🔒 H5 ✉ Campiello del Tintor, San Marco 5513 ☎ 041 523 2205 🕐 Mon–Sat lunch. Closed Sun 🚢 Rialto 1, 2

OSTERIA ALLE TESTIERE €€

www.osterialletestiere.it

One of the top tables in town, if you can get a reservation. The food is inexpensive given the quality that cooking a limited menu for small numbers allows the owner to achieve. The focus is on local dishes, imaginatively prepared and full of zinging tastes.

🔒 J5 ✉ Calle del Mondo Novo, Castello 5801 ☎ 041 522 7220 🕐 Mon–Sat, seatings at 7 and 9.15pm 🚢 Rialto N, 1, 2

OSTERIA L'ORTO DEI MORI €€

There aren't many restaurants in northern Cannaregio, and this is a hit with both locals and tourists. The interior looks as if it's been there for years, with warm panelling and shining glass, but the menu is decidedly 21st century,

EAT

DRINKS

Venice's water is perfectly safe to drink, though Venetians prefer mineral water *(acqua minerale)*—either sparkling *(gassata)* or still *(liscia, naturale* or *non gassata)*. Bottles come in one litre *(un litro* or *una bottiglia)* or half-litre *(mezzo litro* or *mezza bottiglia)* sizes. Bottled fruit juice is *un succo di frutta*, available in pear *(pera)*, apricot *(albiccoca)*, peach *(pesca)* and other tastes. Fresh juice is *una spremuta*, while milk shake is *un frullato*, or *un frappé* if made with ice cream. Lemon soda is a popular and refreshing bitter-lemon drink. Ice is *ghiaccio*, and a slice of lemon is *uno spicchio di limone*.

with Venetian specialities given a modern twist. Everything is well-sourced, short and seasonal; they refuse to use frozen ingredients.

🞣 G2 ⊠ Campo dei Mori, Cannaregio 3386 ☎ 041 524 3677 🕓 Wed–Mon lunch and dinner. Closed Tue 🚢 Orto 41, 42, 51, 52

OSTERIA LA ZUCCA €€

www.lazucca.it

The imaginative and ever-changing food in this pleasantly located *osteria*, especially the vegetable side dishes and main courses, are innovative, at least by Venice's normally conservative standards.

🞣 F4 ⊠ Calle del Tintor (or Tentor), Santa Croce 1762 ☎ 041 524 1570 🕓 Mon–Sat lunch and dinner. Closed Sun 🚢 Riva di Biasio 1, 51, 52

OSTERIA OLIVA NERA €€€

www.osteria-olivanera.com

One of a new breed challenging the old school of Venetian restaurateurs. Its mostly fish and seafood menu shows Venetian cooking can be given a contemporary edge. All fish is fresh from the market. A second restaurant, Oliva Nera II, has opened in the same street at No. 3447 (closed Thursday) offering a more meat-based menu while retaining the same principles of fresh home cooking.

🞣 K6 ⊠ Salizzada dei Greci, Castello 3417–18 ☎ 041 522 2170 🕓 Thu–Tue 12–2.30, 7–10 🚢 Services to San Zaccaria

PAOLIN €–€€

The best café in one of Venice's nicest squares has lots of outside tables and very good ice cream.

🞣 F6 ⊠ Campo Santo Stefano (Campo Francesco Morosini), San Marco 2962 ☎ 041 522 5576 🕓 Daily breakfast, snacks and ice cream. Closed Dec–Jan 🚢 Accademia N, 1, 2

POSTE VECIE €€€

Ingredients could hardly be fresher at this appealing fish restaurant, reputedly founded in 1500, alongside the Pescheria fish market. Cooking is refined, but can be variable, and there's a good wine list.

🞣 H4 ⊠ Campo della Pescaria, San Polo 1608 ☎ 041 721 822 🕓 Wed–Mon lunch and dinner. Closed Tue and 4 weeks in Jul and Aug 🚢 Rialto N, 1, 2, 4

IL REFOLO €

In a quiet corner near a church, this is popular with locals for good pizzas and a limited selection of pastas and main courses.

🞣 F4 ⊠ Campo San Giacomo dell'Olio, Santa Croce 1459 ☎ 041 524 0016 🕓 Tue dinner, Wed–Sun lunch and dinner. Closed Mon and Nov–Mar 🚢 Riva di Biasio or San Stae 1

RIBÓ €€€

This is a refreshingly bright and modern restaurant, serving light and modern Venetian cuisine, and a little off the usual tourist trail. Expect reasonable (though not

---

ETIQUETTE

The procedure when standing up in a bar is to pay for what you want at the cash desk *(la cassa)* and take your receipt *(lo scontrino)* to the bar, where you repeat your order (a tip slapped down on the bar works wonders with the service). Do not then take your drink and sit at an outside table, as you almost always pay a premium to sit down when you order through a waiter. Sitting, a single purchase allows you to relax almost indefinitely.

EAT

inexpensive) prices, superb fresh pasta and fresh fish, and a romantic interior patio garden.

🔲 D5 ✉ Fondamenta Minotto, Santa Croce 158 ☎ 041 524 2486 🕐 Tun–Tue lunch and dinner. Closed Wed and 2 weeks in Aug 🚢 San Basilio N, 2, 61, 62

TAVERNA SAN TROVASO €
www.tavernasantrovaso.it
Not the best cuisine in the city, yet it has reliable cooking and is popular with Venetians. Reserve ahead, (especially for Sunday lunch).

🔲 E7 ✉ Fondamenta Priuli, Dorsoduro 1016 ☎ 041 520 3703 🕐 Tue–Sun lunch and dinner. Closed Mon 🚢 Accademia N, 1, 2

TEAMO €
www.teamo.it
This sleek, relaxing and modern wine bar makes a good change of pace at lunchtime from the traditional Venetian snack bar. There's a wide range of delicious *cichetti* at lunch, including both hot and cold fish- or meat-based dishes, or you could try a platter of mixed smoked meats and cheeses.

🔲 G6 ✉ Rio Terà della Mandola, San Marco 3795 ☎ 041 277 0850 🕐 Daily lunch and snacks 🚢 Giglio 1

TRATTORIA CEA €–€€
This truly Venetian local eating house, and there aren't many left, has been satisfying the neighbourhood for years and you could be the only foreigner in the place. There's a good-value set menu at lunch, or go à la carte and choose from the short menu of mainly fish dishes. If you want to sample *baccalà mantecato* (creamed, dried salt cod), this is the place to try the real thing.

🔲 J4 ✉ Campiello Widmann, Cannaregio 5422/a ☎ 041 523 7540 🕐 Mon–Sat lunch and dinner. Closed Sun
🚢 Fondamente Nove 41, 42, 51, 52

TRATTORIA SAN TOMÀ €–€€
www.trattoriasantoma.com
The pizzas and trattoria food served here are good, but this restaurant's best attraction is its location, only one minute south of Santa Maria Gloriosa dei Frari and the Scuola Grande di San Rocco.

🔲 F5 ✉ Campo San Tomà, San Polo 2864 ☎ 041 523 8819 🕐 Summer daily lunch and dinner; winter Wed–Mon lunch and dinner 🚢 San Tomà N, 1, 2

VINI DA GIGIO €€
www.veneziaristoranti.it
Pretty, relaxed and romantic, this restaurant is on a peaceful canal with two simple beamed rooms and old cabinets. Venetian cooking includes fish and meat dishes, and a short, well-chosen wine list.

🔲 G3 ✉ Fondamenta della Chiesa-San Felice, Cannaregio 3628a ☎ 041 528 5140 🕐 Tue–Sat lunch and dinner, Sun lunch. Closed Mon, Jan and 3 weeks in Aug 🚢 Ca' d'Oro N, 1

EAT

Sleep

Ranging from luxurious and modern upmarket hotels to simple budget hotels, Venice has accommodation to suit everyone. In this section establishments are listed alphabetically.

Introduction

Compared with its population, Venice has more tourist accommodation than any other Italian city. This ranges from 5-star luxury through cutting-edge boutique hotels to low-key, family-run traditional establishments and numerous bed and breakfasts. Despite this, for much of the year Venice remains a seller's market, reflected in the high price of all its accommodation.

What to Expect

Venetian hotels are classified by the Italian state system into five categories from 1- to 5-star (basic to luxury), which reflect facilities rather than room size or decor. Room prices may alter according to the season and all prices must be displayed in the foyer and on the back of bedroom doors; check to see if breakfast is included in this. There are often considerable savings on rack rates by booking online or as part of a package. It's acceptable to ask to see the room; the hotel may have cheaper options than the first room you're shown.

Where to Stay

San Marco has many places to stay and is the heart of the city, but is also very noisy and constantly crowded by day. To the east, Castello is both quieter and cheaper, while to the west Cannaregio has enormous choice, with many budget options near the railway station. Across the Canal Grande, San Polo and Santa Croce have family-run, traditional hotels, particularly around the Rialto, while Dorsoduro, a largely residential area, makes a peaceful choice.

FEELING THE HEAT

Venice is very hot in the summer, so a courtyard or garden is a bonus, as are rooms away from the street. Bear in mind that noise bounces off water and narrow streets, especially if they are major thoroughfares.

From the top: Quatro Fontane hotel; a metal hotel sign; detail of a stained-glass window at the Danieli hotel; a red-carpeted staircase in the luxurious Danieli

SLEEP

Directory

San Marco

Budget
Fiorita
Mid-Range
Al Piave
Flora

San Polo and Santa Croce

Budget
Ai Due Fanali
Ai Tolentini
Alex
Iris

Cannaregio

Mid-Range
Ca' Dogaressa

Castello

Budget
Canada
Doni
Locanda Silva

Mid-Range
Ai Due Principi
Locanda la Corte
Luxury
Danieli

Dorsoduro

Budget
Ca' Foscari
Mid-Range
Accademia-Villa Maravege
American
La Calcina
San Sebastiano Garden
Luxury
Ca' Maria Adele
Centurion Palace
Palazzo Stern

Sleeping A-Z

PRICES

Prices are approximate and based on a double room for one night.

€€€	€351–€800
€€	€176–€350
€	€90–€175

ACCADEMIA-VILLA MARAVEGE €€

www.pensioneaccademia.it

This 17th-century *palazzo*, west of the Accademia, once housed the Russian Embassy. Its 25 rooms are grand and furnished with antiques, although some are small. The garden has a good view of the Canal Grande.

➕ E7 ✉ Fondamenta Bollani, Dorsoduro 1058 ☎ 041 521 0188 🚤 Accademia N, 1, 2

AI DUE FANALI €

www.aiduefanali.com

Set on a tranquil *campo* just back from the Canal Grande, yet only 10 minutes from the station and Piazzale Roma, many of this hotel's comfortable rooms have canal views. Rooms are traditionally furnished, and some are rather small, though they have terracotta and marble bathrooms. There's a roof terrace for summer breakfasts.

E3 ⊠ Campo San Simeon Grande, Santa Croce 946 ☎ 041 18 490 🚤 Riva di Biasio 1, 51,52

AI DUE PRINCIPI €€
www.hotelaidueprincipi.com
The more expensive rooms of this boutique hotel have views over Campo San Zaccaria or the canal in front; they are lofty and spacious with decor that combines traditional Venetian shades with 21st-century design, while the bathrooms are state-of-the-art. The public areas are chic and comfortable and breakfasts are served in a semi-minimalist room.
K6 ⊠ Fondamenta dell'Osmarin, Castello 4972 ☎ 041 241 3979 🚤 Services to San Zaccaria

AI TOLENTINI €
www.albergoaitolentini.it
If you're looking for a simple, excellent-value hotel, the Tolentini, a few minutes' walk from Piazzale Roma, is a good find. The immaculately clean rooms are on the small side, but some have canal views and the beds are comfortable.

Breakfast is not served, but there are bars close by. You can find reduced advance booking rates online; prices plummet in winter.
D5 ⊠ Calle Amai, Santa Croce 197 ☎ 041 275 914 🚤 Services to Piazzale Roma

ALEX €
www.hotelalexinvenice.com
This 1-star hotel, very close to the Frari and San Rocco, offers excellent value. The 11 rooms have been upgraded and redecorated although not all have bathrooms. Breakfast is included in the room price.
F5 ⊠ Rio Terrà Frari, San Polo 2606 ☎ 041 523 1341 🚤 San Tomà N, 1, 2

AL PIAVE €€
www.hotelalpiave.com
This 27-room hotel is located near Campo Santa Maria Formosa and offers good value for Venice. A very sleek, art deco-inspired lobby welcomes guests.
J5 ⊠ Ruga Giuffa, San Marco 4838–50 ☎ 041 528 5174 🚤 San Marco Vallaresso, San Marco Giardinetti, Rialto N, 1, 82

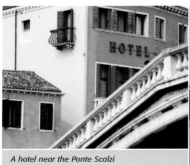

A hotel near the Ponte Scalzi

Many hotels now occupy restored palazzi

SLEEP

AMERICAN €€

www.hotelamerican.com

This 29-room hotel is two minutes' walk from the Accademia, on a small canal away from the crowds. Rooms vary in price and quality but most have wood and period touches. Guests enjoy a terrace and vine-shaded breakfast area.

➕ F7 ✉ Fondamenta Bragadin, Rio di San Vio, Dorsoduro 628 ☎ 041 520 4733 🚤 Accademia N, 1, 2

CA' DOGARESSA €€

www.cadogaressa.com

Ca' Dogaressa is good bet in Cannaregio, where so many hotels are on the busy stretch from the station. The hotel, on the Canale di Cannaregio, has waterside views and the decor of this 18th-century *palazzo* is traditionally Venetian, with beamed ceilings, brocade and Murano glass chandeliers. The owners go out of their way to help guests enjoy Venice, even finding babysitters or booking restaurants.

➕ D2 ✉ Fondamenta di Cannaregio, 1018 Cannaregio ☎ 041 275 9441 🚤 Tre Archi 41, 42, 51, 52

CA' FOSCARI €

www.locandacafoscari.com

This relaxed and well-appointed 1-star hotel has 10 rooms (five with private bathroom) and is hidden away in an alley.

➕ E6 ✉ Calle della Frescada, Dorsoduro

NOISE

Although Venice is remarkably quiet, it still has its fair share of nocturnal traffic—even without cars. Church bells clang through the night and pedestrian chatter in the main alleys and streets is amplified in the close quarters. Traffic on the main canals can also be surprisingly noisy, and refuse boats, *vaporetti* and food suppliers start up very early. This can put a different complexion on that desirable room overlooking the Canal Grande.

3888/b ☎ 041 710 401 🚤 San Tomà or Ca' Rezzonico N, 1, 2

CA' MARIA ADELE €€€

www.camariadele.it

Right next to the Salute and a minute's walk from the *vaporetto*, this luxurious little hotel provides the ultimate in luxurious and romantic living. Choose between one of the themed suites, where the decor ranges from cosy fireside to oriental, or relax in the comfort of a more conventional room. Breakfast is served in a charming room dominated by an over-the-top Murano glass chandelier.

➕ G7 ✉ Rio Terrà dei Catecumeni, 111 Dorsoduro ☎ 041 520 3078 🚤 Salute

LA CALCINA €€

www.lacalcina.com

The waterfront location of this 29-room hotel may not be to all

SLEEP

WHAT'S ON OFFER

Venice offers a huge range of accommodation, and there have been significant changes over the past 10 years. Boutique hotels, small, stylish and chic, arrived around 2000 and there's now a wide choice of hip, and pricey, locations to choose from. At the other end of the scale, bed-and-breakfasts have proliferated everywhere; standards vary so it's wise to research before you book. There's also an increasing number of self-catering flats, bookable via online letting agencies, a good option that gives you more space at lower prices.

tastes, but you are in an interesting area well away from the bustle.
➕ F8 ✉ Fondamenta Zattere ai Gesuati and Fondamenta Vernier, Dorsoduro 780 ☎ 041 520 6466 🚢 Zattere 2, 51, 52, 61, 62

CANADA €
www.canadavenice.com
This immaculate 25-room hotel has several singles. The best room (a double) has its own roof terrace. Reserve in advance.
➕ J5 ✉ Campo San Lio, Castello 5659 ☎ 041 522 9912 🚢 Rialto N, 1, 2, 4

CENTURION PALACE €€€
www.sinahotels.com
In 2009, 5-star luxury came to Dorsoduro when Palazzo Genovese opened after a lengthy restoration. Set where the Canal Grande opens out into the Bacino, the hotel fuses a sensitive reconstruction of a historic building with 21st-century taste and style. Rooms are superbly equipped and comfortable in a modern and individual fashion, while the bar, all-white restaurant and lounges overlook the Canal Grande.
➕ G7 ✉ Campo San Gregorio, Dorsoduro 173 ☎ 041 34281 🚢 Salute

DANIELI €€€
www.luxurycollection.com
A hotel since 1822, the Danieli is the choice of visiting royalty and VIPs. It ranks as the finest of Venice's luxury hotels—but stay in the old wing of the Gothic *palazzo* rather than the newer annexe.
➕ J6 ✉ Riva degli Schiavoni–Calle delle Rasse, Castello 4196 ☎ 041 522 6480 🚢 San Zaccaria 1, 2

DONI €
www.albergodoni.it
An intimate 1-star hotel between the Basilica and San Zaccaria where some of the 13 simple rooms (four with bathroom) overlook the Riva del Vin or the garden.
➕ K6 ✉ Calle del Vin, off Salizzada San Provolo, Castello 4656 ☎ 041 522 4267 🚢 All services to San Zaccaria

FIORITA €
www.locandafiorita.com
This pretty, popular hotel is in a quaint square (used for breakfast in summer) just north of Santo Stefano. The 10 rooms (with private bath) have beamed ceilings.
➕ F6 ✉ Campiello Novo, San Marco 3457/a ☎ 041 523 4754 🚢 Accademia or Sant'Angelo N, 1, 2, 4

FLORA €€
www.hotelflora.it
This 44-room hotel has a well-deserved reputation, thanks to its pleasant garden. Some rooms are rather small. It is just off the south side of Calle Larga (Viale) XXII Marzo west of Piazza San Marco.

RESERVATIONS
It is now almost essential to reserve a room in Venice for July and August, and wise to do so during the rest of the peak season, which officially runs from 15 March to 15 November and from 21 December to 6 January, and now in effect includes the period of *Carnevale* in February. Many hotels do not recognize a low season, however, and lower category hotels where you might have been able to negotiate lower off-season rates often close in winter. Check out the internet for best deals.

➕ G7 ✉ Calle Bergamaschi, San Marco 2283a ☎ 041 520 5844 🚤 Giglio 1

IRIS €

www.hotelirisvenice.com
The Iris is in a quiet area of San Polo near the Frari church. The guest rooms, refurbished in 1997, are light and simply furnished; not all have private bathrooms, but each has a TV, hairdryer and telephone; some have canal views.
➕ E5 ✉ Fondamenta dei Forner, Calle del Cristo, San Polo 2910/a ☎ 041 522 2882 🚤 San Tomà

LOCANDA LA CORTE €€

www.locandalacorte.it
This delightful hotel was home to a Venetian noble family in the 16th century, and its 16 rooms maintain a historic and luxurious look but with modern amenities. The inner courtyard, where breakfast is taken, is a special treat.
➕ J5 ✉ Calle Bressana, Castello 6317 ☎ 041 241 1300 🚤 Fondamente Nove 52

LOCANDA SILVA €

www.locandasilva.it
The Silva is in a lively *calle* between Santa Maria Formosa and San Marco. The public areas, including the breakfast room, have modern furniture and fittings, while bedrooms are light, modern and functional. Some have pleasant

canal views and the cheapest share a bathroom.
➕ J5 ✉ Fondamenta di Remedio, Castello 4423 ☎ 041 522 7643 🚤 Services to San Zaccaria

PALAZZO STERN €€–€€€

www.palazzostern.com
For a room with a view, check into the Stern, one of Venice's prettiest Gothic Canal Grande *palazzi*. The breakfast terrace is set on the water; inside, an overhaul restored the interior to its Gothic-Moorish appearance, the work of the 19th-century owner. Rooms are traditionally furnished in Venetian style, and there's a rooftop Jacuzzi with great city views.
➕ E6 ✉ Calle del Traghetto, Dorsoduro 2792/a ☎ 041 277 0869 🚤 Ca'Rezzonico 1

SAN SEBASTIANO GARDEN €€

www.hotelsansebastianogarden.com
Tucked away on a quiet canal just back from the Giudecca canal, this comfortable hotel is housed in a thoughtfully renovated old *palazzo*. All is space and calm in the public areas, while the bedrooms are large, traditionally decorated and comfortable. The chief draw, perhaps, is the garden, a lovely green space.
➕ D6 ✉ Fondamenta San Sebastiano, Dorsoduro 2542 ☎ 041 523 1233 🚤 San Basilio 2, 8, 61 62

SLEEP

Need to Know

**This section takes you through all the
practical aspects of your trip to make it run
more smoothly and to give you confidence
before you go and while you are there.**

NEED TO KNOW

Planning Ahead

WHEN TO GO

Avoid July and August, the hottest and busiest months, and plan a visit for April (excluding the busy Easter period), May, June, September or October. Hotels are busy from Easter to October, in February during Carnevale, and over Christmas and New Year. Despite the weather, winter can still be a delightful time to see the city.

TIME

Italy is one hour ahead of GMT in winter, six hours ahead of New York and nine hours ahead of Los Angeles.

TEMPERATURE

JAN	FEB	MAR	APR	MAY	JUN	JUL	AUG	SEP	OCT	NOV	DEC
43°F	46°F	59°F	66°F	73°F	74°F	79°F	79°F	70°F	61°F	54°F	45°F
6°C	8°C	12°C	15°C	20°C	23°C	26°C	25°C	21°C	16°C	12°C	7°C

Spring (March to May) has a mixture of sunshine and showers, the chill easterly wind, the *bora*, can lower temperatures. Fog occurs occasionally.

Summer (June to August) can be unpredictable; clear skies and searing heat one day followed by sultry clouds and thunderstorms the next.

Autumn (September to November) can be glorious, though be prepared for wet days and *acqua alta* (peak tides). November is often wet and foggy with high *acqua alta*.

Winter (December to February) *Acqua alta* can occur at any time (including into March); January and early February can be bitterly cold with brilliant sunshine.

WHAT'S ON

February *Carnevale* (carnival): pageants, masks and costumes.

March *Su e zo per i ponti*: A long road race in which competitors run 'up and down the bridges' of Venice (fourth Sunday in Lent).

April *Festa di San Marco*: A gondola race from Sant'Elena to the Punta della Dogana marks the feast day of Venice's patron saint. Men traditionally give women a red rose.

May *La Sensa*: Venice's mayor re-enacts the Marriage to the Sea, in which the doge would cast a ring into the sea to symbolize the 'wedding' of the city to the sea (Sunday after Ascension Day). *Vogalonga*: Literally the 'long row', a 32km (20-mile) race from Piazza San Marco to Burano and back (one Sunday in May).

June *Biennale*: Venice's international art exhibition (Jun–Nov) is in odd-numbered years; architectural Biennale in even-numbered years.

July *Festa del Redentore*: Pontoons are laid across the Giudecca canal to the Redentore to celebrate Venice's deliverance from the plague of 1576. People picnic in boats and watch fireworks (third Sunday of the month).

September *Venice Film Festival*: Held on the Lido (late Aug/early Sep). *Regata Storica*: Historical costume pageant and procession of boats on the Canal Grande, followed by a race among gondoliers (first Sunday of the month).

November *Festa della Salute*: A pontoon is built across the Canal Grande, to the Salute, to celebrate the passing of a plague in 1630 (21 Nov).

VENICE ONLINE

www.enit.it
The main Italian Tourist Board website carries a wealth of information on everything you need to know about the whole country, with Venice getting plenty of attention. The site is available in several languages.

www.veniceconnected.com
Advance booking, reduced-price, official site for transportation, sightseeing and everything you'll need. Prices fluctuate according to how busy the city will be during your visit, and all services on offer are optional, enabling you to build your own package. Book seven days in advance and collect your tickets on arrival.

www.turismovenezia.it
This excellent site, in English and Italian, gives a wealth of information on every aspect of the city. You'll find details of accommodation, restaurants and shopping as well as the full lowdown on what to see and do. There's a frequently updated newsletter and good links to other sites.

www.comune.venezia.it
Although aimed as much at local residents as visitors, the city council's site provides good up-to-date information on cultural activities and historic sites in the city. Look here for the latest on erratically opening museums, city services and what's on when. The site is linked to www.veniceconnected.com.

www.venezia.net
Italian site with English version. News, general travel information, shopping, a selection of bars, cafés and restaurants, excellent material on museums and main attractions, plus 3-D tours of sights.

www.hellovenezia.it
Use this site before you go to buy travel and event tickets, purchase the VeniceCard, which offers reductions on both travel and entry tickets, and check route maps and timetables.

GOOD TRAVEL SITES

www.actv.it
Venice's city transportation system runs this informative site where you'll find full route details, timetables and fare structures for the *vaporetto* network.

www.trenitalia.com
The official site of the Italian State Railways with excellent train information and an easy-to-use search facility—good for forward planning.

www.museiciviciveneziani.it
Everything about Venice's museums, including the collections, opening times, prices and facilities.

www.fodors.com
A travel-planning site where you can research prices and weather, book tickets, cars and rooms, and ask fellow travellers questions; links to other sites.

INTERNET ACCESS

As well as internet access in many hotels and internet cafés, Venice now has WiFi access at hot spots all over the city, which are mapped at www.cittadinanzadigitale.it/node/67. To use these, pay online and obtain a username and password from www.veniceconnected.com. Twenty-four hour access costs €5, 72 hours €8, and seven days €15.

Getting There

ENTRY REQUIREMENTS

For the latest passport and visa information, look up the British embassy website at www.ukinitaly.fco.gov.uk or the United States embassy at www.usembassy.gov. EU citizens can obtain health care with the production of the EHIC card. However, insurance to cover illness and theft is strongly advised.

ARRIVING BY CAR

Cars must be left at one of the multi-storey car parks at the Tronchetto (linked by boat 2 to the rest of the city) or the more central Piazzale Roma, from where you can walk or catch boats N, 1, 2, 41, 42, 51, 52, 61, DM (Diretto Murano). Rates start at about €26 a day. There are no free car parks and no other parking places; cars parked elsewhere will be towed away and in summer, long lines on the causeway approaching the city are common. Consider leaving your car in Mestre and then taking the train.

AIRPORTS

There are direct flights to Venice from all over the world. Venice has two main airports, Marco Polo and Canova in Treviso.

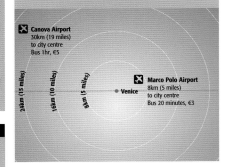

Canova Airport
30km (19 miles)
to city centre
Bus 1hr, €5

Marco Polo Airport
8km (5 miles)
to city centre
Bus 20 minutes, €3

24km (15 miles)
16km (10 miles)
8km (5 miles)
Venice

FROM MARCO POLO

Scheduled internal and international flights (plus a few charters) arrive at Venice's Marco Polo Airport, 8km (5 miles) north of the city hub. For flight information, tel 041 260 9260; www.veniceairport.it. Connections from Marco Polo to Piazzale Roma take 20–40 minutes and can be made by taxi, blue ATVO Fly/35 bus (www.atvo.it; every 30 minutes 8.10am–11.40pm, to 12.20am on Sat; €3 one-way) or less expensive ACTV No. 5 orange city buses (www.actv.it; 4.08am–1.10am; €2 one-way). Buy tickets for buses from the automatic ticket machines in the baggage reclaim area, in the arrivals hall or next to the bus stop. Buses leave from the concourse outside the terminal.

BY WATER FROM SAN MARCO

There are two options: a regular boat service, run by Alilaguna, or the more expensive option, the water taxi. To get to the boats take the shuttle bus *(navetta)*, which runs regularly every 5 to 10 minutes to the lagoon edge. If you want to walk down, it's a 7- to 12-minute walk turning left outside the terminal building. The cheaper option is run by the Società Alilaguna (tel 041 240 1701;

www.alilaguna.com) with an hourly boat service from Marco Polo to the city. It costs €13 and goes to San Marco, the Lido and Zattere. Make sure you buy your ticket before you leave the airport, the office is close to the arrivals hall exit.

Of the four lines, the Linea Alilaguna Rossa goes via Murano, the Lido, Arsenale and San Marco to the Zattere and on to the Hilton on the Giudecca; and the Linea Alilaguna Blu travels via Murano, the Fondamente Nuove and the Lido to San Zaccaria and San Marco. Choose the service that will take you as near as possible to your hotel; you may find that you will have to connect with an ACTV *vaporetto* for the last stages. The Blu (blue) services start at 6.10am; thereafter the boat leaves at 7.10, then hourly at 10 minutes past the hour until 3.15pm. The Rossa (red) boats start at 9.15am and run hourly until 15 minutes past midnight. Tickets cost €13 and can be bought on board; the journey time is around 75 to 90 minutes. A third line, the Oro (gold) goes directly to San Marco (hourly 8.30–3.30pm). The fourth Aranria (orange) line runs to Murano, Madonna dell' Orto and Guglie at 9.55am then hourly until 3.55pm.

Water taxis are run by the Consorzio Motoscafi Venezia, whose desk is to the left of the exit from the baggage reclaim area in the Marco Polo airport arrivals hall (tel 041 522 2303; www.motoscafivenezia.it). The taxis run to most points within the city (20 minutes), but the prices are high (officially €50 but baggage surcharges can easily double this).

FROM TREVISO

Treviso airport (tel 0422 315 111 or 0422 315 1312; www.trevisoairport.it), 30km (19 miles) outside the city, is served by low-cost airlines; a ATVO/Eurobus shuttle (www.atvo.it; €5 each way) connects with some of these. Buy tickets at the ATVO ticket office or foreign exchange outlet.

ARRIVING BY TRAIN

Trains to Venice arrive at the Venezia Santa Lucia station, often abbreviated as Venezia SL (☎ 89 20 21 or 199 892 021; from outside Italy 0039 06 684 75475; www.trenitalia.it). The station is at the head of the Canal Grande, five minutes' walk from Piazzale Roma; from the quays outside there are frequent *vaporetto* (1, 2 and others) and *motoscafo* (52) boat services to the rest of the city. Be sure the boat you board is heading in the right direction. Many through trains stop on the mainland at Mestre station (☎ 041 929 472), confusingly called Venezia Mestre (Venezia M), without continuing to Venice proper. Check your train is destined for Santa Lucia; if not, catch one of the frequent connecting services at Mestre for the 15-minute trip across the causeway.

GETTING TO YOUR HOTEL

Before you leave, ask your hotel to send you details of how to reach them. You need to know the nearest *vaporetto* stop, the name of the street as well as the *numero civico* (the number given after the district in the address), and the nearest landmark, such as a *campo*, church or museum.

Getting Around

HANDY HINT

Tourist tickets are available for ACTV boats. A 12-hour ticket costs €16, 24-hour €18, 36-hour €23, 72-hour €33 and 7-day €50. Buy tickets online at www.venice connected.com, at the ACTV offices at Piazzale Roma and Tronchetto and other important *vaporetto* stops.

VISITORS WITH DISABILITIES

Venice is difficult for visitors with disabilities. Streets are narrow, there are numerous bridges and moving on and off boats is almost impossible. Hotels, galleries and other public spaces are often in historic buildings where conservation restrictions limit access. This said, matters are improving, and the Venetian and Italian state tourist offices have lists of suitable hotels and contact details of Italian associations for those with disabilities.

GONDOLAS

Hiring a gondola is enchanting, but expensive (starting at around €80 for 40 minutes). Rates are negotiable, so confirm the cost and duration before departure. Do not be afraid to walk away or haggle if the prices seem too high and there are plenty of gondoliers. If cost is an issue take the cheap public gondalas, the *traghetti*.

NEED TO KNOW

The best way to move around Venice is on foot; this is how the Venetians themselves get from place to place, combining walking with the judicious use of public transportation in the shape of *vaporetti* (water buses) and *traghetti* (cross-Canal Grande ferries).

BOATS

● ACTV runs two basic types of boat: the general-purpose *vaporetto* and the faster *motoscafi*. Both follow set routes and are numbered at the front of the boat. As the same number boat may run in two directions it is vital at the quays—which have separate boarding points for each direction—to make sure you board a boat heading the right way. This is particularly true at the Ferrovia and San Zaccaria—both are busy terminals for several routes.

● The web of boat routes around Venice is not as confusing as it first seems. The basic route is Line 1 along the Canal Grande (Piazzale Roma–Vallaresso–Lido and back). Line 2 also follows the Canal Grande, but has fewer stops. A second 2 boat runs from San Zaccaria to Piazzale Roma by way of the Giudecca. The other boat you may use is the Laguna Nord (LN), which runs to the islands of Murano and Burano from the Fondamente Nuove. The 'T' shuttle connects Burano and Torcello. The ferry information throughout this guide gives the nearest stop as well as the line number.

● Tickets can be bought at most landing stages, on board boats (with a surcharge), and at shops or tobacconists with an ACTV sticker. One-way tickets (€6.50, valid for 60 minutes) are valid along the length of the route so the price is the same for one stop or 10 stops. Tickets must be validated by passing them in front of the I-Mob electronic scanner before boarding; a green light will show. If you have a tourist ticket this must be validated every time you use it. There are spot fines for riding without a ticket.

● Special tickets are available (▷ panel).

● ACTV runs a less frequent service with a

reduced number of stops throughout the night on key Canal Grande routes (indicated by 'N' throughout the guide). Exact times are posted on the timetables at every quay. Tickets can be bought on board.

TAXIS

● For rides to and from the mainland there are taxi stands at Piazzale Roma, tel 041 595 2080; Marco Polo Airport, tel 041 541 6363; and Mestre rail station, tel 041 936 222. Otherwise, call Radio Taxi, tel 041 595 2080.

TRAGHETTI

● As there are only four main bridges across the Canal Grande, Venice's *traghetti* (ferries) provide an invaluable service. Think of them as bridges and it becomes clear they will save both time and unnecessary mileage. They exist primarily for the convenience of locals, but once you are familiar with the system, judicious use of the *traghetti* will help you get quickly from point to point. Using large gondolas, they ply back and forth at seven strategic points. Quays are usually obscure, so look for the little yellow 'Traghetto' signs. Crossings cost around €0.60, which you hand to the ferryman as you board. Venetians usually stand, but nobody minds if you sit unless the boat is crowded. Be careful with small children, and watch your balance when the boat pushes off.

WATER TAXIS

● Venice's water taxis *(motoscafi)* are fast but extremely expensive (▷ 164–165). The basic rate is €18 when the clock starts, and €1.30 per minute after that. Surcharges are levied for each piece of luggage for trips on public holidays and between 10pm and 7am, and for each additional passenger over a maximum of four. You can hail a taxi on a canal, but it is usually easier to call by phone—which means about €15 on the clock before you start, tel 041 723112 (San Polo), 041 522 2303 (San Marco), 041 715787 (Cannaregio), 041 966170 (airport), 041 718235 (Santa Lucia rail station).

TOURIST INFORMATION

● Main tourist offices
☎ 041 529 8711 (all offices);
www.turismovenezia.it
✚ H7 ✉ Venice Pavilion, Palazzina del Santi by the Giardinetti Reali ⏰ Daily 10–6
✚ H6 ✉ Piazza San Marco 71/f (Ascensione) ⏰ Daily 9–3.30
● Train station ✚ D4
⏰ Daily 8–6.30
● Marco Polo Airport office
⏰ Daily 9.30–7.30
● Lido office ✉ Gran Viale Santa Maria Elisabetta 6
⏰ Summer only 9.30–12.30, 3.30–6
● Piazzale Roma office
✚ D5 ✉ Garage ⏰ Daily 9.30–6.30

LOST PROPERTY

● City streets ☎ 041 274 8023 or visit Vigili Urbani office in Pizzale Roma
● Buses or boats ☎ 041 272 2179 or 041 2424
⏰ Mon–Sat 8–6/4.30 in winter
● Train or station
☎ 041 785 531
● Report lost passports to the police and your consulate
● Report general losses to Questura, the main police
✉ Fondamenta Santa Chiara, Santa Croce 500
☎ 041 271 5772

Essential Facts

EMBASSIES AND CONSULATES

● France ✉ (Honorary Consul), Palazzo Morosini, Calle del Pestina, Castello 6140 ☎ 041 522 4319
● Netherlands ✉ San Vidal, San Marco 2888 ☎ 041 528 3416
● Republic of Ireland ✉ Piazza San Pietro in Gessate 2, Milano 20122 ☎ 02 551 8756
● UK ✉ Via San Paolo 7, 1-20121 Milan ☎ 02 723 001
● USA ✉ Via Principe Amedeo 2/10, Milano 20121 ☎ 02 290 351

ELECTRICITY

● Current is 220 volts AC (50 cycles), but is suitable for 240-volt appliances.
● Plugs are the continental two-round-pin.

EMERGENCY PHONE NUMBERS

● Emergency services (police, fire and ambulance), tel 113
● Police (Carabinieri), tel 112
● Questura (Venice Police Station), tel 041 271 5772
● Fire (Vigili di Fuoco), tel 113 or 115
● Ambulance, tel 041 523 0000 or 118
● Hospital and first aid (Ospedale Civile) at Campo SS Giovani e Paolo, tel 041 5239 4517

MONEY

● The euro is the official currency of Italy. Bank notes in denominations of 5, 10, 20, 50, 100, 200 and 500 euros, and coins in denominations of 1, 2, 5, 10, 20 and 50 cents and 1 and 2 euros were introduced on 1 January 2002.
● Foreign-exchange facilities are available at banks and kiosks throughout the city. Major credit cards are widely accepted in Venice and can be used in ATMs displaying the appropriate sign.

NATIONAL HOLIDAYS

● 1 Jan: New Year's Day; 6 Jan: Epiphany; Easter Monday; 25 Apr: Liberation Day; 1 May: Labour Day; 2 Jun: Republic Day; 15 Aug: Assumption; 1 Nov: All Saints' Day; 8 Dec: Immaculate Conception; 25 Dec: Christmas Day; 26 Dec: Santo Stefano

OPENING HOURS

● Banks: Mon–Fri 8–1.30 (larger branches also 3–4 and resricted Sat opening).
● Churches: Non fixed hours but generally Mon–Sat 9–12, 3–6, Sun 1–5; except St. Mark's and those in the Chorus Group (▷ 4) scheme.
● Shops: Generally daily 9–1, 4–8 or 9.30/ 10–7.30/8; most food shops close Wed

afternoons except in summer; other shops
close Monday mornings except in summer.

POST OFFICES
● Venice's central post office *(posta* or *ufficio postale)* is near the Rialto bridge (Palazzo delle Poste, Fondaco dei Tedeschi, San Marco 5554, tel 041 271 7111; www.poste.it; Mon–Sat 8.30–6.30
● Stamps *(francobolli)* are available from post offices and *tabacchi* displaying a large 'T' sign.
● Mailboxes are red or blue and are marked *Poste* or *Lettere*. Blue boxes are for faster and more expensive *posta prioritaria* services only.

SENSIBLE PRECAUTIONS
● Venice's tourists are a target for theft, but with a few precautions you can stay safe. Report thefts to your hotel and then to the main police station. Report lost passports to the police or embassy.

TELEPHONES
● Telecom Italia (TI) provides public telephones in bars, on the streets and in TI offices. All are indicated by red or yellow signs showing a telephone dial and receiver. Venice has TI booths in Piazzale Roma, open 8am–9.30pm; and the main post office.
● Public phones accept coins and most accept phone cards *(schede telefoniche)*, available from tobacco shops, TI offices, automatic dispensers or stores displaying a TI sticker.
● The area code for Venice is 041 and must be used when calling from outside and within Venice.

TOILETS
● Venice has public toilets at the rail station and in larger museums. There are public toilets throughout the city marked with blue and green signs. Most cost €1 and some have attendants to give change if needed.
● In bars and cafés ask for *il gabinetto* or *il bagno*. Do not confuse *signori* (men) with *signore* (women).

HEALTH
● Likely hazards include too much sun, air pollution and biting insects.
● Water is safe to drink unless marked *acqua non potabile*.
● Pharmacies *(una farmacia)* are identified by a green cross and have the same opening hours as shops, but open late on some days as displayed on pharmacy doors. Staff can give advice on minor ailments and dispense many medicines over the counter, including some only available by prescription in other countries. Remember to bring any prescriptions that might be required to obtain medicine.
● If you wish to see a doctor *(un medico)*, ask at your hotel. For first aid *(pronto soccorso)* or hospital treatment, visit the Ospedale Civile ➕ J4 ✉ Campo Santi Giovanni e Paolo, Castello ☎ 041 5239 4517

ETIQUETTE
● In churches do not wear shorts or miniskirts and cover your arms.
● Do not intrude while church services are in progress.
● Do not eat or drink in churches. Many churches and galleries forbid flash photography, or ban photography altogether.

Words and Phrases

All Italian words are pronounced as written, with each vowel and consonant sounded. Only the letter h is silent, but it modifies the sound of other letters. The letter c is hard, as in English 'cat', except when followed by i or e, when it becomes the soft ch of 'cello'. Similarly, g is soft (as in the English 'giant') when followed by i or e—*giardino, gelati*; otherwise hard (as in 'gas')—*gatto*. Words ending in o are almost always masculine in gender (plural: -i); those ending in a are generally feminine (plural: -e). Use the polite second person *(lei)* to speak to strangers and the informal second person *(tu)* to friends or children.

USEFUL WORDS	
yes	*sì*
no	*no*
please	*per favore*
thank you	*grazie*
you're welcome	*prego*
excuse me!	*scusi*
where	*dove*
here	*qui*
there	*là*
when	*quando*
now	*adesso*
later	*più tardi*
why	*perchè*
who	*chi*
may I/can I	*posso*
good morning	*buon giorno*
good afternoon/ good evening	*buona sera*
good night	*buona notte*
hello/good-bye (informal)	*ciao*
hello (on the telephone)	*pronto*
I'm sorry	*mi dispiace*
left/right	*sinistra/destra*
open/closed	*aperto/chiuso*
good/bad	*buono/cattivo*
big/small	*grande/piccolo*
with/without	*con/senza*
more/less	*più/meno*
hot/cold	*caldo/freddo*
early/late	*presto/ritardo*
today/tomorrow	*oggi/domani*
when?/do you have?	*quando?/avete?*

NUMBERS	
1	*uno, una*
2	*due*
3	*tre*
4	*quattro*
5	*cinque*
6	*sei*
7	*sette*
8	*otto*
9	*nove*
10	*dieci*
20	*venti*
30	*trenta*
40	*quaranta*
50	*cinquanta*
100	*cento*
1,000	*mille*

COLOURS	
black	*nero*
brown	*marrone*
pink	*rosa*
red	*rosso*
orange	*arancia*
yellow	*giallo*
green	*verde*
light blue	*celeste*
sky blue	*azzurro*
purple	*viola*
white	*bianco*
grey	*grigio*

NEED TO KNOW

EMERGENCIES

help!	*aiuto!*
stop, thief!	*al ladro!*
can you help me, please?	*può aiutarmi, per favore?*
call the police/an ambulance	*chiami la polizia/ un'ambulanza*
I have lost my wallet/ passport	*ho perso il portafoglio/il passaporto*
where is the police station?	*dov'è il commissariato?*
where is the hospital?	*dov'è l'ospedale?*
I don't feel well	*non mi sento bene*
first aid	*pronto soc corso*

USEFUL PHRASES

How are you? (informal)	*Come va?*
I'm fine	*Sto bene*
I do not understand	*Non ho capito*
Do you speak English?	*Parla Inglese?*
How much is it?	*Quant'è?*
Do you have a room?	*Avete camere libere?*
Can I see the room?	*Posso vedere la stanza?*
I have a reservation	*Ho una prenotazione*
How much per night?	*Quanto costa una notte?*
... with bath/shower	*... con vasca/doccia*
When is breakfast served?	*A che ora è servita la colazione?*
Where is the train/bus station?	*Dov'è la stazione ferroviaria degli autobus*
Where are we?	*Dove siamo?*
Do I have to get off here?	*Devo scendere qui?*
I'm looking for ...	*Cerco ...*
Where can I buy ...?	*Dove posso comprare ...?*
A table for ... please	*Un tavolo per ... per favore*
I'm a vegetarian	*Sono vegetariano/a*
Is there a house specialty?	*C'è uns specialità della casa?*
The bill, please	*Il conto, per favore*
We didn't have this	*Non abbiamo avuto questo*
Where are the toilets?	*Dove sono i bagni?*

DAYS/MONTHS

Monday	*lunedì*
Tuesday	*martedì*
Wednesday	*mercoledì*
Thursday	*giovedì*
Friday	*venerdì*
Saturday	*sabato*
Sunday	*domenica*
January	*gennaio*
February	*febbraio*
March	*marzo*
April	*aprile*
May	*maggio*
June	*giugno*
July	*luglio*
August	*agosto*
September	*settembre*
October	*ottobre*
November	*novembre*
December	*dicembre*

TIME AND PLACE

morning	*mattina*
afternoon	*pomeriggio*
evening	*sera*
night	*notte*
today	*oggi*
tomorrow	*domani*
yesterday	*ieri*
early	*presto*
late	*tardi*
later	*piu tardi*
when	*quando*
where	*dove*
Where is...?	*Dov' è...?*
Where are we?	*Dove siamo?*
here	*qui/qua*
there	*li/là*
near	*vicino*
far	*lontano*
on the right	*a destra*
on the left	*a sinistra*

Index

The Automobile Association would like to thank the following photographers, companies and picture libraries for their assistance in the preparation of this book.

Abbreviations for the picture credits are as follows: (t) top; (b) bottom; (l) left; (r) right; (c) centre; (AA) AA World Travel Library.

2(i) LOOK Die Bildagentur der Fotografen GmbH/Alamy; **2(ii)** Beren Patterson/Alamy; **2(iii)** Nic Cleave Photography/Alamy; **2(iv)** Alessandro Villa/Alamy; **2(v)** imagebroker/Alamy; **3(i)** AA/A Mockford & N Bonetti; **3(ii)** Matthew Kawalski/Alamy; **3(iii)** Kumar Sriskandan/Alamy; **3(iv)** Jim Ritchie/Alamy; **4** AA/A Mockford & N Bonetti; **5** LOOK Die Bildagentur der Fotografen GmbH/Alamy; **6/7t** CHRISTOPHE SIMON/AFP/Getty Images; **6ct** an Dagnall/Alamy; **6cb** travelstock44/Alamy; **7ct** Travelshots.com/Alamy; **7cb** AA/A Mockford & N Bonetti; **6/7b** AA/S McBride; **8/9t** Gaertner/Alamy; **8ct** AA/A Mockford & N Bonetti; **8cb** Alberto Paredes/Alamy; **8b** petforsberg/Alamy; **9ct, 9cb** AA/A Mockford & N Bonetti; **9b** Food Features/Alamy; **10l** AA, **10r** MBP-one/Alamy; **11l** AA; **11r** MARKA/Alamy; **12** Beren Patterson/Alamy; **14l** Paul Carstairs/Alamy; **14/15l** AA/C Sawyer; **15tr, 15br** AA/A Mockford & N Bonetti; **16l** Peter Howard Smith/Alamy; **16/17t, 16/17b, 17r** AA/A Mockford & N Bonetti; **18/19** The Art Archive/Alamy; **19r** Andrea Matone/Alamy; **20l** AA/S McBride; **20/21** AA/R Newton; **21r** AA/C Sawyer; **22l, 22/23t, 22/23b, 23br** © The Peggy Guggenheim Collection, Venice. Photo: Andrea Sarti/CAST1466; **24l, 24/25, 25tr, 25br** AA/A Mockford & N Bonetti; **26/27** John Kellerman/Alamy; **27** AA/D Miterdiri; **28/29** John Kellerman/Alamy; **29tr** Adam Eastland Italy/Alamy; **29br** Chuck Pefley/Alamy; **30l** The Art Archive/Alamy; **30/31** Hackenberg-Photo-Cologne/Alamy; **31r** AA/D Miterdiri; **32l, 32tr, 32/33b, 33tl, 33r** AA/A Mockford & N Bonetti; **34l** AA/S McBride; **34/35** AA/A Mockford & N Bonetti; **35r** AA/A Mockford & N Bonetti; **36l** © Maurizio Cattelan/Marian Goodman Gallery. Photo by Vittorio Zunino Celotto/Getty Images; **36/37** (c) Charles Ray/Courtesy Matthew Marks Gallery, New York. Photo by Jevgenija Pigozne/Photolibrary Group; **37r** Luca Da Ros/SIME/4Corners; **38** Biblio Photography/Alamy; **38/39, 39tr, 39br** AA/A Mockford & N Bonetti; **40/41** Vincent MacNamara/Alamy; **41r** Angelo Hornak/Alamy; **42l** AA/A Mockford & N Bonetti; **42/43** AA/S McBride; **43tr, 43br** AA/A Mockford & N Bonetti; **44l** AA/D Miterdiri; **44tr, 44/45b** AA/C Sawyer; **45tl** AA/A Mockford & N Bonetti; **45r** Roberto Esposti/Alamy; **46/47** AA/A Mockford & N Bonetti; **47r** Worldwide Picture Library/Alamy; **48tl, 48bl, 48/49** AA/C Sawyer; **49r** AA/S McBride; **50/51** AA/A Mockford & N Bonetti; **51r** adam eastland/Alamy; **52l** John Kellerman /Alamy; **52/53** AA/C Sawyer; **53tr, 53br** AA/A Mockford & N Bonetti; **54l** AA/R Newton; **54/55** AA/S McBride; **56/57** AA/A Mockford & N Bonetti; **57r** Michael Harding/Alamy; **58l** AA/D Miterdiri; **58/59, 59tr** AA/A Mockford & Bonetti; **59br** Lonely Planet Images/Alamy; **60/61** Marka/Alamy; **61tr, 61br, 62l, 62tr, 62/63, 63tl, 63tr, 63br** AA/A Mockford & N Bonetti; **64** Nic Cleave Photography/Alamy; **66** CuboImages srl/Alamy; **67l** John Kellerman/Alamy; **67r** AA/A Mockford & N Bonetti; **68l** KC Hunter B/Alamy; **68r** Collpicto/Alamy; **69l** Stefan Nielsen/Alamy; **69r** The Art Archive/Alamy; **70l** F1online digitale Bildagentur GmbH/Alamy; **70r** AA/A Mockford & N Bonetti; **71l** Chuck Pefley/Alamy; **71r, 72** AA/A Mockford & N Bonetti; **73l** David Tomlinson/Alamy; **73r** AA/A Mockford & N Bonetti; **74** Nic Cleave Photography/Alamy; **75l** F1online digitale Bildagentur GmbH/Alamy; **75r** Chris Howarth/Italy/Alamy; **76** Yannis Larios/Alamy; **77** Giovanni Tagini/Alamy; **78** funkyfood London - Paul Williams/Alamy; **79** Stock Italia/Alamy; **80** Alessandro Villa/Alamy; **82t** Dave Pattison/Alamy; **82b** AA/A Mockford & N Bonetti; **83t** Ian Dagnall/Alamy; **83b** B&Y Photography/Alamy; **86(i)** Chris Selby/Alamy; **86(ii)** John Kellerman/Alamy; **86(iii)** Julian Wyth/Alamy; **86(iv)** Andrea Matone/Alamy; **86(v)** Jon Arnold Images Ltd/Alamy; **88t** Petr Svarc/Alamy; **88b** Lonely Planet Images/Alamy; **89t** Martyn Vickery/Alamy; **89c** John Kellerman/Alamy; **92t** Peter Barritt/Alamy; **92c** Paul Carstairs/Alamy; **92b** Ian Fraser/Alamy; **93** BANANA PANCAKE/Alamy; **94t** Lonely Planet Images/Alamy; **94b** petforsberg/Alamy; **95t** Paul Carstairs/Alamy; **95c** Jorge Fernandez/Alamy; **95b** CuboImages srl/Alamy; **98(i)** Ross Warner/Alamy; **98(ii)** Adam Eastland Italy/Alamy; **98(iii)** Adam Eastland Italy/Alamy; **98(iv)** AA/A Mockford & N Bonetti; **99** Matteo Colombo/Alamy; **100t** Radius Images/Alamy; **100b** LOOK Die Bildagentur der Fotografen GmbH/Alamy; **101t** CuboImages srl/Alamy; **101c** Sarah Quill/Alamy; **104t** AA/A Mockford & N Bonetti; **104c** Chuck Pefley/Alamy; **104b** AA/D Miterdiri; **106t** Geoff A Howard/Alamy; **106b** Alessandro Villa/Alamy; **107t** AA/S McBride; **107c** oliver selwyn/Alamy; **107b** LOOK Die Bildagentur der Fotografen GmbH/Alamy; **110(i)** AA/C Sawyer; **110(ii)** CuboImages srl/Alamy; **110(iii)** AA/A Mockford & N Bonetti; **110(iv)** imagebroker/Alamy; **110(v)** AA/A Mockford & N Bonetti; **110(vi)** OpenPhoto/Alamy; **110(vii)** AA/A Mockford & N Bonetti; **112t** I CAPTURE PHOTOGRAPHY/Alamy; **112b** LOOK Die Bildagentur der Fotografen GmbH/Alamy; **113t** LOOK Die Bildagentur der Fotografen GmbH/Alamy; **113b** AA/A Mockford & N Bonetti; **116t** giuseppe masci/Alamy; **116c** Ivan Vdovin/Alamy; **116b** AA/A Mockford & N Bonetti; **117** Images Etc Ltd/Alamy; **118** imagebroker/Alamy; **120/121t, 120/121cb, 120/121, 120/121cb, 120/121b** AA/A Mockford & N Bonetti; **120/121b** Ian Dagnall/Alamy; **121ct** ENP/Alamy; **121cb** AA/A Mockford & N Bonetti; **123** CuboImages srl/Alamy; **126, 130** AA/A Mockford & N Bonetti; **132/133t** Cris Haigh/Alamy; **132/133ct, 132/133cb** AA/A Mockford & N Bonetti; **132/133b** JTB Photo Communications, Inc./Alamy; **133ct** AA/R Newton; **133cb** Paul Carstairs/Alamy; **138** Terry Smith Images/Alamy; **140** Matthew Kawalski/Alamy; **142t** Kevin Galvin/Alamy; **142ct** Bon Appetit/Alamy; **142cb** Chuck Pefley/Alamy; **142b** AA/A Mockford & N Bonetti; **145l** MARKOS DOLOPIKOS/Alamy; **145r, 148** Bon Appetit/Alamy; **152** Kumar Sriskandan/Alamy; **154t, 154ct** AA/A Mockford & N Bonetti; **154cb** AA/D Miterdiri; **154b** Hemis/Alamy; **156l** ENP/Alamy; **156r** Adam Eastland Italy/Alamy; **160** Jim Ritchie/Alamy.

Every effort has been made to trace the copyright holders, and we apologise in advance for any unintentional omissions or errors. We would be pleased to apply any corrections in a following edition of this publication.

174

Venice's 25 Best

WRITTEN BY Tim Jepson
ADDITIONAL WRITING BY Sally Roy
SERIES EDITOR Marie-Claire Jefferies
REVIEWING EDITOR Linda Schmidt
PROJECT EDITOR Bookwork Creative Associates Ltd
COVER DESIGN Guido Caroti
DESIGN WORK Lesley Mitchell
INDEXER Marie Lorimer
PICTURE RESEARCHER Michelle Aylott
IMAGE RETOUCHING AND REPRO Jacqueline Street

ISBN 978-1-4000-0551-2

EIGHTH EDITION

IMPORTANT TIP
Time inevitably brings changes, so always confirm prices, travel facts, and other perishable information when it matters. Although Fodor's cannot accept responsibility for errors, you can use this guide in the confidence that we have taken every care to ensure its accuracy.

SPECIAL SALES
This book is available for special discounts for bulk purchases for sales promotions or premiums. Special editions, including personalized covers, excerpts of existing books, and corporate imprints, can be created in large quantities for special needs. For more information, write to Special Markets/Premium Sales, 1745 Broadway, 3-2, New York, NY 10019 or email specialmarkets@randomhouse.com.

Color separation by AA Digital Department
Printed and bound by Leo Paper Products, China

10 9 8 7 6 5 4 3 2 1

Cover image: Paul Reid/Shutterstock

A04634
Maps in this title produced from map data © New Holland Publishing (South Africa) (Pty) Ltd, 2009
Transport map © Communicarta Ltd, UK